The Unofficial Masterbuilt Smoker Cookbook

A BBQ Smoking Guide
&
100 Electric Smoker Recipes

MW00949276

Legal Disclaimer

THIS BOOK IS NOT AFFILIATED WITH MASTERBUILT®.

The information contained in this book is the opinion of the author and is based on the author's personal experience and observations. The author does not assume any liability whatsoever for the use of or inability to use any or all information contained in this book, and accepts no responsibility for any loss or damages of any kind that may be incurred by the reader as a result of actions arising from the use of information in this book. Use this information at your own risk. The author reserves the right to make any changes he or she deems necessary to future versions of the publication to ensure its accuracy.

SMOKIN' BOB JENSEN IS JUST A REGULAR FAN....WHO HAPPENS TO COOK GREAT BBQ.

Smokin' Bob loves hearing from his fans. Here is some contact info to keep handy:
Official Masterbuilt: www.masterbuilt.com | customerservice@masterbuilt.com
Smokin' Bob: www.smokeandgrillmeat.com || smokeandgrillmeat@gmail.com

WANT TO KNOW HOW TO COOK THE WORLD'S MOST FLAVORFUL AND TENDER MEAT?

GET THE QUICKSTART GUIDE FREE!

This book comes with a barbecue grilling quickstart guide which includes:

- Recipes for finger lickin' good sauces and rubs
- Time and temperature guide to cooking any type of meat
- More secrets and techniques straight from the pros
- All new upcoming high-quality guides

**GRAB YOUR FREEBIES NOW AT
SMOKEANDGRILLMEAT.COM**

Southern barbecue is the closest thing we have in the U.S. to Europe's wines or cheeses; drive a hundred miles and the barbecue changes.

— *John Shelton Reed*

Contents

MEAT GRILLING GUIDE

Whatever type of meat you're cooking,
the following tips will add much more flavor to your dish:

1. Avoid using metal pieces like spatulas to prevent the nonstick surface from chipping away and getting in your food.

2. After searing or panfrying the meat, remove it from the pan and save the fat drippings and crispy bits (these bits are loaded with flavor and can be easily stirred into homemade sauces).

3. Generously brush vegetables and meats with seasonings, olive oil or melted butter to add more flavor or healthy fats to your diet.

4. To get the fantastic smoky flavor of an open flame barbecue, try adding a little liquid smoke to your marinade.

5. Always cut open the meat to look inside and check for doneness. Poultry should turn white from pink all throughout, while beef looks dark brown.

6. You get the best results from pounding the meat down to about ¾ in. thick. Boneless cuts of meat that are uniformly thick will brown evenly and cook inside properly.

7. A brine is a salt water solution that keeps meats like chicken breasts moist and juicy. 2-3 hours in a flavored brine solution can add intense flavor and keep the meat tender.

BEEF: Some cuts of beef are naturally ideal for cooking on an indoor grill, like ribeye steak for example. As long as the cut is tender and uniformly thick, it will cook evenly and thoroughly.

Type of cut	Method	Heat	Grilling Time (covered)	Internal Temp (min)
Steak (¾ in. thick)	Direct	High	4-7min (Medium rare) 6-8min (Medium) 8-10min (Well done)	145°F (63°C) 160°F (71°C) 170°F (77°C)
Steak (1 ½ in. thick)	Direct	High	5-8min (Medium rare) 7-9min (Medium) 9-11min (Well done)	145°F (63°C) 160°F (71°C) 170°F (77°C)
Kabobs	Direct	High	5-7min	145°F (63°C)
Hamburger patties (½ in. thick)	Direct	High	5-7min	145°F (63°C)

CHICKEN AND POULTRY:

Using rubs and glazes to cook poultry are a really great way to add flavor quickly. To prevent the meat from drying out, some people recommend using the indoor grill for the lovely grill marks and flavor on the outside, but to finish cooking the inside in an oven for about 8-10 minutes.

Type of cut	Method	Heat	Grilling Time (covered)	Internal Temp (min)
Chicken breast (6-8 oz.)	Direct	Medium-High	8-12min	170°F (77°C)
Wings (4 oz.)	Direct	High	8-12min	170°F (77°C)
Kabobs	Direct	High	10-15min	170°F (77°C)
Chicken patties (½ in. thick)	Direct	High	10-15min	170°F (77°C)
Turkey breast	Direct	High	10-15min	170°F (77°C)

SEAFOOD:

Fish cooks quickly when using direct heat. Once removed from the grill, let it sit for a few minutes to let the outer crust form. Once the crust has formed, it can be easily flipped over without sticking or falling apart.

Type of cut	Method	Heat	Grilling Time (covered)	Internal Temp (min)
Fillets (½ in. 1 in.)	Direct	Medium-High	3-5min	170°F (77°C)
Shrimp	Direct	High	3-5min	170°F (77°C)

VEGETABLES: Thoroughly rinse, trim, and chop up vegetables to have them ready to go. Some of these vegetables require precooking before grilling.

To precook, simply boil a saucepan of water and add vegetables. Set on simmer, and cover for the recommended times from the chart below.

Vegetable	Precook	Method	Heat	Grilling time (covered)
Asparagus	3min	Direct	Medium-High	3-5min
Eggplant	No	Direct	High	5-7min
Onions	No	Direct	High	6-8min
Leeks	8min	Direct	High	3-5min
Mushrooms	No	Direct	High	4-6min
Potatoes	8-10min	Direct	High	6-8min

Part 1 Where There's Fire, There's Smoke

Introduction

Civilization began when humans discovered fire.

For thousands of years, humans cooked their food over fires, whether outdoors or on kitchen hearths. And for thousands of years, those same people had the same problem—how to preserve the "leftovers," and store food against the lean times of winter or famine. The use of salt and smoke to preserve food dates back to prehistory. And while other methods of cooking and preserving have come along, it's probably fair to say that when humans colonize the rest of the galaxy, someone's going to bring along a grill.

This book is offered as an introductory guide to the art and science of smoking food both to enhance its flavor and preserve it. You'll find the basics here—from how to choose the best smokers to the pros and cons of smoking methods. We even address the age-old controversy: *to soak or not to soak?*

We'll share all our best tips and techniques and last but not least, provide you with a collection of recipes that are so tasty you'll want to use your smoker every day. Are you all fired up? Then let's begin.

Special Health Bonus

Preparing your own smoked foods, so long as you work with unprocessed ingredients, allows you to avoid the harmful additives (nitrates and nitrites) found in commercially prepared smoked foods. Since these additives have positively been linked to health issues including dementia and Alzheimer's, DIY smoking seems like the way to go.

Smokeology 101

For many years, smoking food was a necessity—hunters needed a way to preserve whatever parts of the animal couldn't be consumed immediately—

and the delicious taste imparted by smoking was just a bonus. But as society moved away from the hunter-gatherer model (became more "civilized"), smoked foods gradually became prized, even coveted, for their taste. Before refrigeration, the only way a diner who lived far inland could enjoy seafood was in its smoked or dried form. But even smoked foods had to be moved great distances, adding transportation costs to the final price, which is how smoked oysters became a luxury item available only to the wealthy few.

The modern era of smoking food primarily for flavor dates back only to the first part of the 20th century when the Torry Kiln was invented in Scotland. This device could be temperature-controlled, allowing for large quantities of meat to be smoked with uniform results. In the 70 years since that invention, smoker technology has gone high-tech and low-tech and practically no-tech in its innovations. No matter what you want to smoke; no matter what kind of fuel you have available; this is a cooking technique that you can use. But first…let us define some terms.

How to Talk the Talk

As with any vocation or avocation, the art of smoking comes complete with its own lexicon of terms and the first thing you need to know is the difference between barbecuing, grilling, and smoking. First of all, even though "barbecue" and "grill" are often used interchangeably, they're not quite the same thing. And although you can use a grill as a smoker, and barbecued meat is flavored by smoke, smoking and grilling aren't the same thing either.

But it's not as complicated as it sounds. The basic rule of thumb is: Grilling is fast and hot while smoking is slow and low.

Barbecuing is usually done on a grill, but when you "barbecue" food, you cook it at a lower temperature (around 300-500 degrees Fahrenheit) than when you grill food. **Grilling** is a high-heat (above 500 degrees), quick-cooking method that sears the outside of the meat and seals the juices inside.

Smoking, on the other hand, is usually a low-heat (under 140 degrees) process of exposing ingredients to smoke. It is a process that can take hours, or as long as several weeks, to complete.

The exception is **"Hot Smoking,"** which is a method that roasts and flavors the meat simultaneously at temperatures above 140 degrees. Food that is "hot smoked" is fully cooked.

"Cold Smoked" food, usually cheese (which will ooze and melt at higher temperatures) or fish is prepared at a much lower temperature, typically between 68-90 degrees Fahrenheit.

Here are a few other smoking terms you might encounter in conversations:

AMNPS—is the patented shorthand for the Amaze-N-Pellet Smoker, a portable smoke generator that burns either sawdust or pellets (which are made from compressed sawdust) and works for both cold and hot smoking.

Bark—the crunchy, fatty crust that develops on the outside of meat when it's heated past 300 degrees, setting off the "Maillard Reaction."

Brine—is a salting process that is either a "wet brine" (salt mixed with water and sometimes spices) or "dry" (salt rubbed into the food). Brining meat (particularly poultry) will help keep it moist during the smoking process.

Chimney—a cylindrical device used to help ignite charcoal without lighter fluid, which can add toxic chemicals to smoke and a terrible taste to the meat.

COS—Cheapo Offset Smoker. (See EOS.)

Dalmatian Rub—salt and pepper.

EOS—refers to an Expensive Offset Smoker (See COS.)

Gasser—A derogatory term for propane-fueled smokers, usually uttered by those who think that using electric- and gas-fueled smokers is "cheating."

L.P.—liquid propane gas used to fuel grills and smokers. Usually available in 20-lb. bottles.

Maillard Reaction—a chemical process that occurs between 285-330 degrees Fahrenheit when foods are browned. This process is responsible for the crunchy layer (known as "bark" among barbecue enthusiasts) that forms on the outside of a seared piece of meat as the golden-brown crust on baked bread.

Montreal-style smoked meat—is made by salting beef brisket and curing it with salt and spices then hot-smoked and steamed. It is similar to pastrami and served in much the same manner.

Reverse Sear—using indirect heat to raise the temperature in the center of a piece of meat.

Smoke Point—the point at which fat begins to smoke; will vary according to substance. Butter has a low smoke point (around 325 degrees) while ghee (clarified butter) has a smoke point of 485 degrees.

Stick burner—a smoker that is designed to use burning logs as fuel.

When You're Ready to Make the Investment

Buying a smoker and accessories is considerably more expensive than buying a backyard barbecue and some long-handled tongs. Choosing the right smoker for your needs depends on a number of factors so before you buy, ask yourself these questions:

How much do I want to spend? Depending on your needs, a smoker can run you anywhere from under $500 to $10,000 and up.

How much space do I have? Side Offset smokers require more room and are a lot less portable than smokers with a vertical design.

How much will I use it? If you just want to smoke a turkey for the holidays or make the occasional pulled pork sandwich, your best bet is probably one of the indoor stove-top smokers that are user-friendly and inexpensive. If your lifestyle includes a lot of outdoor parties or big family gatherings, you might want to invest in a "big rig" that offers rotisserie and other options for making smoked meat for a crowd.

How much time do I have to devote to smoking? Smokers that require wood or charcoal as fuel are more labor-intensive and require more supervision than electric or gas smokers.

Am I interested in doing this competitively? We're not talking about the friendly (or not-so-friendly) neighborhood competition over who makes the best smoked beef but the actual barbecue/smoker circuit where there's not just bragging rights on the line but cash as well. The circuit has its own subculture (which puts Burning Man's "burners" to shame) and spectacle.

Amazing Ribs has a list of the country's biggest smoker/barbecue bashes here:
http://amazingribs.com/bbq_competitions/barbecue_competitions_and_associations.html

The Right Tools for the Job

Just as you wouldn't hand the keys to a high-end sports car to a kid with a learner's permit, you don't need a fully loaded grilling gizmo if you're just starting out. Patience is the secret to the success of smoking food and while becoming a pitmaster may not take as long as mastering a foreign language, you need to learn to walk before you can run. It will only frustrate you if you buy a smoker that is more than you can handle.

Using The Masterbuilt®'s Digital Controls

To set temperature:
1. Press on button.
2. Press SET TEMP button after LED display blinks to life.
3. Use the "+/-" to set temperature.
4. Press SET TEMP again to finalize temperature selection.

To set timer:
1. Press SET TIME button after LED display for hours blinks
2. Use the "+/-" to set temperature.
3. Press SET TIME Button again to lock in I was selected. Next the minutes section will start blinking
4. Use the "+/-" to set temperature.
5. Press SET TIME to lock in minutes and start the cooking cycle.

To use meat probe:
1. Insert meat probe right into the center of meat to get an accurate reading.
2. Press and hold MEAT PROBE button, and the LED display will reveal the internal tem-

perature of the meat being probed.

3. Once MEAT PROBE button is released-LED display will return to set temperature or set time.

To use light:

1. Press LIGHT button to switch light on.
2. Press LIGHT button to switch light off.

To RESET control panel:

If control panel shows an error message, turn electric smoker off, unplug unit from outlet, wait ten seconds, plug unit back into outlet, then turn electric smoker on. This will reset control panel.

The "Sweet & Simple" Masterbuilt® Quickstart Guide

One reason the Masterbuilt® Smoker is so popular is because of its ease of use. The main advantage to this machine is it's "set-it-and-forget-it" functionality. Yes, you should be responsible and check on it every now and then. But this is a slow smoker, so give it plenty of time to cook and you will certainly enjoy the results.

In order to preseason the smoker:

Fill it with a handful of woodchips and set it to its highest temperature with air vents completely open.

Let it burn for about two hours, and add woodchips once again during the entire process.

Feel free to use various types of woodchips to get different smoky flavors: hickory, apple, pecan, and mesquite are quite popular.

Sometimes the meat reaches the desired temperature before you're ready to serve. If this case, wrap it in aluminum foil and reduce the temperature until it is time to eat.

Do not overload the smoke. You will cause uneven cooking and extended cooking time more than necessary. The best cooking method is to allow proper heat circulation.

If you want to apply barbecue sauce or other wet ingredients, apply the sauce to the meat an hour before it is finished cooking and then wrap with foil.

Dry rubs are okay to apply to the meat before being placed in the smoker.

Do not cover the racks with aluminum foil since this will prevent heat from circulating inside effectively.

Masterbuilt® Reviews

We poured through hundreds of reviews online and compiled a condensed list of things that people either love or hate about the Masterbuilt® Smoker.

Things People Love:

1. The handheld remote control is a super convenient feature. It will allow you to program the time and temperature and check the meat probe temperature.
2. Solid construction. The machine is well-built and the material used is high quality.
3. Great for cooking for lots of people as there is a lot of room inside.
4. Ease of use. Because this machine is digital, it is very easy to monitor and check up on. Great for beginners or advanced barbecue aficionados.
5. Very economical. It runs on electricity and with small amounts of wood, relatively speaking.

You can save a lot of money in the long run if you smoke a lot of meat.

Common Complaints:
1. Barbecue purists say you're losing something by not burning a real wood or charcoal fire. This smoker does not replace a high heat grill like a gas grill. (But you can always finish off the smoked meat in a gas grill if you have one)
2. Many people complain about the smoke tray not working correctly no matter what they tried. (This can be solved by requesting a retrofit kit from Masterbuilt®, which they should send for free if you are in the warranty period)
3. Several people have been complaining that their machine stop working after only a few uses. (However, their customer service seems quite responsive and willing to help you solve all issues)
4. The heat retention is a common problem. But this issue exists for virtually every smoker or grill on the market. Opening the door for even a few seconds can cause the internal temperature to drop by 50° or more immediately.
5. Over time, the machine can develop a metallic smell that affects the smoke. Some people report that this machine gives a smoky/metallic odor.

Smokers Best Suited for the Adventurous Amateur
Vertical Box Smokers

These are simple in construction and stable. Prices can vary and on the lower end of the price range, the boxes may not be as well insulated, resulting in temperature fluctuations. If you have a choice between a vertical box smoker and a vertical water smoker at roughly the same price, most experts will tell you to go for the water smoker.

Pros: Portability, especially in comparison with often unwieldy offset smokers.
Cons: They are not as versatile as other smokers and in particular make poor grills. It can also be harder to access the meat while it's cooking.

Water Smokers

These smokers are built with three basic elements—a chamber for the fuel source, a water pan, and then space for the food you're smoking.

Vertical Water Smokers are the cheapest smokers you can buy. (One of the most popular brands sells for less than $100) and overall, these are the best-selling smokers on the market. They are also relatively easy to use. They can be fueled by charcoal, electricity or a gas burner, and all that's necessary is to fill the water pan and then ignite or turn on the fuel source. Add the meat and that's it.

Pros: These smokers are small and take up relatively little real estate. They are also more fuel efficient than larger smokers.
Cons: When using a small water smoker you cannot regulate the smoke as well as you can in other kinds of smokers so there's more of a danger of creosote building up on your smoked food.

Offset Barrel Smokers

These smokers can be tricky for novices, so you should probably have some pit-time under your belt before you purchase one. They are fueled with wood or charcoal.

Offset barrel smokers, also known as "pipe smokers," "horizontal smokers," or "stick-burners" used to dominate competition smoking/barbecue events. In an "offset" smoker, the firebox is set lower (or sometimes, in back) of the cooking chamber where the food is being smoked. This means the heat is not directly under the food but next to it.

Brinkmann makes several versions of their Offset smoker and all of them come in at under $300, which makes this type of smoker one of the most affordable. On the downside, some users have complained that the more inexpensively priced smokers are too small for big jobs, like smoking a turkey.

High-end offset smokers ($800 and up) are

made of thicker metal and will provide a low, even, radiant heat.

Pros: Offset smokers allow you to smoke larger cuts of meat than a vertical smoker. Offset smokers can also be used as grills while vertical smokers are not really meant for that task.

Cons: More inexpensive brands of offset smokers tend to have leaky fireboxes that can make it difficult to control airflow. Other reported problems include a tendency for the paint to flake and the metal to rust.

Kamado-Style Smokers

These were inspired by traditional wood/charcoal-burning cookers (originally clay pots) used in Japan for centuries, these modern-day smokers are made out of a variety of materials including ceramics, steel, terracotta, and a mixture of cement and crushed rock. The ubiquitous BGE (Big Green Egg) is one of the best-known smokers of this type.

Pros: The sophisticated venting system allows for precision air flow. Fans of this style of smoker praise its versatility. The construction allows for intense heat (up to 750 degrees) so that in addition to grilling and smoking, you can even bake.

Cons: Price. These smokers are expensive; with price tags that start at just under a thousand and go up to what you might expect to pay for a used car.

Don't Try This At Home: Industrial Smokers

Industrial smoker ovens are the ovens you see in the back of shacks with pigs on the roof. (According to food writer Calvin Trillin, you can never go wrong eating at a place decorated with a plastic animal.) These smokers are fueled by or gas and may be mobile. The three things to consider when choosing an Industrial smoker are: capacity needs, kitchen space, and budget. In general, electric-powered industrial smokers are smaller; mobile rigs are usually fueled by natural gas or propane.

You can't buy these bad boys at just any barbecue store, but there are a number of companies like Cookshack that can supply them. They're also frequently available on eBay, priced at between $8500-$10,000.

Useful Tools for the Smoker

A fire extinguisher

Every home should have one and you should never embark on a smoking project without one. You should have a fire extinguisher that is rated ABC— that is, capable of extinguishing Class A fires (those that burn flammables like paper and wood); Class B fires (grease and oil, which are not extinguished with plain water); and Class C (electrical fires). These are dry chemical extinguishers that need to be inspected on a yearly basis.

A meat thermometer

If you buy only one barbecue/smoking accessory it should be a high-quality thermometer, especially if you're using an inexpensive water smoker that doesn't allow you to regulate the smoker's temperature. The state of the art as far as thermometers go

is the **Thermapen**, which retails for around $100.

Fuel + Wood = Smoky Deliciousness

It's all fuel for the fire, but wood comes in all sorts of states. Each has its virtues and its pitfalls.

Charcoal

Not all charcoal is created equal. In its simplest form, "charcoal" is simply the carbon residue left behind when any organic material (wood, coconut shell, bone) is heated in the absence of air. Commercial charcoal is available as lumps, briquettes (pillow shaped or hexagonal), or extruded forms. **"Lump" charcoal** is made directly from hardwood without preservatives and produces far less ash than the other forms of charcoal. It burns hotter than briquettes but also burns out faster.

Lump charcoal commonly comes in mesquite, hickory, and oak varieties and which you choose depends on which flavor you want to add to your food. Aromatic mesquite, for instance, often provides a smoky subtlety to Tex-Mex and Southwestern barbecue. Of the three options, mesquite is probably the "most potent," and can be used to impart flavor to meats that cook quicker. Oak has a flavor that enhances the flavors of game, red meat, and oily fish like shad, mackerel, and bluefish. Hickory is hands down the most popular wood used for smoking in both its charcoal and plank form. It is the dominant flavor note in dishes like pulled pork, and "hickory smoked" flavor is added to everything from baked beans to bottled ketchup.

For a comparison of the lump charcoals available to the serious smoker, consult The Naked Whiz' Lump Charcoal Database

The ubiquitous pillow-shaped briquettes commonly seen at backyard barbecues are made of a mix of compressed charcoal made from sawdust and other wood byproducts with a binder of some sort. Most commercial brands also contain fillers and additives.

Hexagonal charcoal is made from compressing charcoal without binders and while it works for regular barbecues (and is used by street vendors all over the Far East), it is virtually odorless and smokeless and burns for less than four hours, so it is useless as fuel for a smoker.

You might have to special-order it, but there are briquettes that are 100 percent hardwood or mostly wood with only cornstarch or wheat paste as a binder.

Extruded charcoal is made from raw ground wood or carbonized wood. The heat and pressure of the extrusion process holds the charcoal together in log-shaped pieces.

Coconut shells—not just for serving umbrella drinks any more.

There are several brands of charcoal briquettes on the market that are made out of coconut shells. Advertised as sustainable and environmentally friendly, coconut shell briquettes burn hot and long, and produce very little ash, with no coconut taste. The briquettes are more expensive than more conventional type of briquette, but when you use them, you know you're not getting any toxic chemicals in your smoke along with the flavor you crave.

Storing Charcoal Safely

There's an enduring myth that wet charcoal can "spontaneously" combust and is thus a fire hazard. This misconception apparently began with a misinterpretation of fire hazard data (mostly pertaining to coal going back to the 1950s.

Scientists who've studied the origin of fires attributed to "spontaneous combustion" of wet charcoal concluded that the small quantities of charcoal stored in the average-size bag of commercially available charcoal could NOT spontaneously combust at ambient temperatures below 250 degrees Fahrenheit.

Still, that doesn't mean you shouldn't use common sense. Charcoal should be stored in a dry, well-ventilated space away from potential ignition sources. It should be protected from the elements.

Logs, Planks, Chunks, and Chips

If you decide to go old school and fire up your smoker with wood, you have some choices to make and some questions to ask:

Can you use any kind of wood in a smoker/barbecue? No. Soft woods like pine not only burn too quickly but they'll also ruin the flavor of your food as the aromatic resins in the wood evaporate into the smoke. Not only that, but the sticky residue the atomized resins leave behind will ruin the insides of your smoker. Stick to hard woods like oak, hickory, maple, and mesquite.

Which is better, chips or chunks? Most experienced pit-masters will say chunks are best. You can use up a whole bag of chips in the same amount of time that three or four medium-sized chunks of hardwood burn.

Is it really necessary to soak wood/chips before using them? Conventional wisdom—and a lot of old books on smokeology—insist that you absolutely must soak chips and chunks of wood. In the old days, before grills and smokers allowed for more reliable temperatures, soaking wood kept it from catching on fire and ruining the food with creosote and other deposits. Now—especially with gas and electric smokers—that danger is almost nonexistent and even in wood-fueled smokers, chips and chunks in well-insulated fire pans or in a foil pouch, should not catch fire.

What's the most flavorful wood to use? We've all seen "Applewood smoked" bacon on menus and in

the gourmet meat section of the supermarket, but applewood (which is also really good for smoking chicken and poultry) isn't the only fruit wood that you can throw on the fire to add flavor.

If you don't have access to chunks of wood to flavor your fire, you can buy bags of "Smoking Chips" or "BBQ Chips," which come in a wide variety, including cherry, peach, orange, lemon, and even avocado. More traditional types of chips include mesquite, alder, maple, pecan, hickory, and oak. If you can't find what you need locally, try a source like: Wholesale Patio Store

Plank Smoking

Plank smoking is an indirect cooking method. The food (most commonly fish or game, but now any kind of meat or poultry as well) is placed on a plank and then cooked to the side of the heat source. In contradiction to the "rule" about never using soft wood for smoking, planks are most commonly made of soft cedar wood because the cooks want the strong aromatic cedar wood taste to flavor the food.

This method of cooking food was traditionally used among Native Americans in the Pacific Northwest where salmon and other fish were a primary food source but it's since been incorporated into every corner of the U.S., including Virginia, where an annual "shad planking" event is a political hot ticket.

Indoor Smoking

It's not always practical to smoke food outdoors. Maybe it's too cold or too rainy or you live in an area like drought-stricken Southern California where total fire bans are in effect through most of the summer. Maybe you live in an urban high-rise apartment without a yard.

Safety First

If you've ever cooked fried chicken in a cast-iron skillet, you know that the process can kick up so much smoke that you'll be tempted to disconnect your smoke alarm.

You may worry that indoor smoking is messy or downright dangerous. Just be sure to follow the directions on whatever device you're using for your indoor smoking and make sure the kitchen fan is on!

Kitchen Magic: Turn Your Stove Into a Smoker

Stove-top kettle smokers look like big Dutch ovens with domed lids. They fit directly over the stove's heating element (and will work with gas, electric, and glass-top stoves). They are priced at about what you'd pay for a high-end skillet, around $75.

These smokers have a space inside for the flavoring wood and a rack for holding the food you're smoking. (With some models customers have complained the rack is really hard to remove.) Some kettle smokers are big enough for a water pan as well. Once they're loaded, follow the directions included with the smoker, set the vent and go about your business.

Things to watch out for: If you're using a stove-top smoker for a long period of time, make sure the chips don't get black and burn. Not only is that a fire risk, but burned wood will leave creosote deposits on the food. If you see the wood chips starting to get black, just scoop them out and put in new ones.

Also, though you can use these smokers with both dry and wet heat, you will get more flavor from the smoke if you "dry smoke" it in this type of smoker.

Part 2

Tips and Techniques

Turn Your Oven Into a Smoker

This is an incredibly easy way to smoke food and it doesn't require much in the way of "extras."

First, preheat your oven to 250 degrees Fahrenheit. Line the bottom of a large aluminum roasting pan with a single layer of wood chips that have been soaked in water and then drained. Add enough extra water so that there is a thin layer of water between the pan and the chips.

Add a metal roasting rack to the pan. (Using a turkey roasting pan/rack is perfect here.) Add the meat to the rack. Make sure the meat is over the wood chips, which it should be if there is a layer of chips across the bottom of the pan.

Tip: Do not stack the wood chips. They will generate too much smoke (leaving creosote on the meat) if they are stacked together.

Seal the pan on all sides with foil, but leave a hole at the top for venting the smoke. Put the pan of chips and meat in the oven and leave for 2-3 hours, depending on the weight of the meat you're smoking.

Check to see that the chips don't get too dried out and add more water if necessary.

Grilling Papers

Despite the name, grilling "papers" are actually thin, pliable strips of wood that are soaked and then wrapped around food before it's put into the pan.

It's in the Bag

Most veteran cooks know that roasting meat in a bag will lock in moisture and prevent such failures as a bone-dry Thanksgiving turkey. Now you can buy "smoking bags" that come with wood chips (in a variety of flavors) already enclosed. They're easy to use and not terribly expensive—around $5 each. You can even buy smoker bags filled with chips from the oak barrels Jim Beam uses to age its bourbon

Almost nobody does it right the first time. As with stoves, smokers all have their little quirks and it's only when you start using them that you learn what those quirks are. There are thriving online communities that host forums and blogs and sites that can help you out, though, and if you can think of the question, someone out there will have an answer. (It might not be an informed answer—smoking meat seems to evoke such high passions that it's best to get a second opinion on controversial matters.) But below are some of the tips and techniques we've collected in our years of cooking with fire.

First-Timer "Newbie" Rules

1. Always be careful what you put around a hot cooking device like the Masterbuilt® Smoker.
   - Pay attention to loose clothing, children, body parts, or any items near the grill -- especially when in the grill is in use
2. The smoker can be heavy. Be very careful not to drop it on your damn foot.
   - Don't even try to move the smoker when it's fired up. I shouldn't have to tell you this, but you never know these days with things like Youtube…
3. Do NOT put your smoker on top of a wooden surface or other combustible materials.
   - Keep in mind that a lot of heat is generated from the bottom of the grill and surrounding objects could potentially get damaged or catch on fire.
4. When the Masterbuilt® smoker is not in use,

do not leave the door open. Moisture and rain will ruin the cooking device. Then you will have to go buy a new one.
5. Lighter fluid is definitely not recommended for this smoker. It seeps into the metal and can taint your machine and any food that you cook in it.
6. For your first time use, do not cook at high temperatures yet!
   - It is recommended to stay below 350°F / 177°C
7. Never QUICKLY open the door all the way. You could seriously burn yourself with flashes of intense heat that escape the smoker immediately.

Did You Just Buy A New Smoker?
1. Calibrate new smokers by doing a couple "dry runs" without any food. You will remove all traces of metal shavings, dust, grease, and other things that naturally build up during the manufacturing and shipping process.
2. Wipe down the inside and outside of the smoker thoroughly with soap and warm water.
3. Then spray the interior with vegetable oil, throw in some wood (8-10 oz) and light for 30 min.

Guide to Hot Smoking Times and Temperatures

The Official Meat Smoking Calculator online is a quick resource for times and temperatures required to smoke everything from chicken legs to competition ribs.

http://meatsmokingcalculator.com/

Below is a chart that will give you guidelines for the most popular meats you might want to smoke. All temperatures are in given in Fahrenheit.

Always use a meat thermometer to decide if a food is thoroughly cooked. You can't go by "eye" alone as smoked meat will often darken during the process. Applewood smoking, in fact, will impart a reddish hue to chicken.

Meat	Smoking Temp (Fahrenheit)	Cooking Time	Final Temp (Fahrenheit)
Baby Back Ribs	225-240	5-6 hrs	Tender*
Beef Ribs	225	3-4 hrs	175
Brisket (Whole)	225	1.25 hrs/pound	185
Chicken (Whole)	250	4 hrs	165
Chicken (Breasts)	250	1.25	165
Chicken (Thighs)	250	1.5 hrs	165
Pork Butt (Pulled)	225	1.5 hrs/pound	205
Salmon	140-160	5-7 hrs	145
Spare Ribs	225-240	6-7 hrs	180
Turkey (Whole, 12 lbs.)	275**	6.5 hrs	165
Turkey (Leg)	250	4 hrs	165
Turkey (Wings)	225	2.5 hrs	165
Turkey Breast (bone in)	240	4-6 hrs	165

* You can't easily use a meat thermometer on Baby Back Ribs to tell if they're done so you will probably need to try the "separation test." This means lifting the entire rack of meat off the cooking rack with your tongs. If it cracks, it's likely done. You can also test for meat color. The meat should be mostly white, with just a little pink under the skin. And there shouldn't be any liquid.

** This is a higher temperature than some smokers suggest, but it will allow the smoked turkey skin to get crispier. If it starts to get too dark, cover with aluminum foil.

The Only Tips You Need for Smoking:

1. Cook the raw meat early to let the it absorb the flavor compounds in smoke fully. Smoke does not penetrate well when the surface cools and dries out.
2. Real traditional barbecue is cooked low and slow. Indirect heat with wood smoke is the best way to make tough meats moist and tender.
3. Water pans are great for maintaining heat. Too much fluctuation in temperature can cause rubbery and dry food. If cooking longer than an hour with charcoal, use a water pan to stabilize the heat.
4. A common mistake new smokers make is adding too much wood or charcoal. A general rule is to smoke food no longer than half its cooking time.
5. Black smoke is bad! White smoke is good. Keep your fire well ventilated.
6. Keep the air flowing. Be sure to open the vents to allow the smoke to swirl over the food, flavoring it properly and to exit through the top.
7. Do not leave the smoker unattended! Seriously, you could burn or ruin your food in a matter of minutes for many reasons without proper supervision. Or worse, start a dangerous fire.
8. Don't keep peeking. Each time you open the lid, you let precious heat and smoke escape. Only open the lid when you need to tend to the fire, coals, or food.
9. Well-barbecued meat is supposed to shimmer with a dark-brown crust that almost looks black. Known as "bark," it is the delicious result of sizzling fat and spices with smoke on the meat's surface.

So You Screwed Up. What Went Wrong?

Why does my smoked meat taste bitter? If your meat is bitter, it means that there's a creosote (black tar) buildup on the meat created by poor airflow or smoke that's too heavy. Make sure your smoker is clean and that it's venting properly.

My smoked meat went bad. How did that happen? Smoking, like salting (or "curing"), used to be a method of preserving food before refrigeration and there's a widespread belief that simply smoking food will keep it edible at room temperature. **Don't believe it.**

If meat has simply been smoked or wet-cured, it will start to go bad after just a few hours at room temperature. (The bacteria that cause spoilage thrive in moisture.) It will keep for several days if refrigerated, and up to several months if wrapped properly and frozen.

Dry-cured, smoked meats like "country hams" or dried Italian sausage will keep unrefrigerated for years until they're cut into because harmful bacteria can't reproduce without moisture. Once that protective "bacteria barrier" has been cracked, however, the food can absorb moisture from air and should be refrigerated.

A special note about home-made jerky: Commercially produced jerky has a very long shelf life but the home-made version tends to absorb moisture. It should be eaten within a month.

Signs that smoked meat has gone bad:

It has a foul odor.
It is moist, or even slimy.
It changes color.
It has mold growing on it. (Note: salt-cured "country hams" often have mold on their "rinds" but that's not cause for alarm.)

General Food Safety

Common sense is your best ally in making certain your food is safe. Always make sure your food preparation area is clean. Wash your hands before handling raw meat, particularly chicken, which is notorious for being an incubator of bad bacteria.

Sterilize cutting boards and wash knives between uses.

When storing smoked food in the freezer, make certain that it's wrapped in air-tight packages.

Cold Smoking Safety Basics

When being cold smoked, food must show a core temperature of 140 degrees for a full minute to make certain that foodborne parasites like ringworm and tapeworm are killed. If the cold smoking process has been combined with salting, it may still not be enough to kill off all parasites. The FDA recommends freezing food (particularly salmon) at a temperature of minus 4 degrees Fahrenheit to kill these parasites.

The Pantry/Fridge

Although the advent of electric and gas smokers has made smoking a less labor-intensive endeavor, smoking a cut of meat or a slab of fish, or a hunk of cheese is not something most people do on the spur of the moment. Still, if you happen to have any of the following ingredients on hand, you're halfway there.

Cheese

Now that artisanal cheeses have become popular, it's possible to find smoked cheese in varieties other than cheddar and Gouda. You can smoke almost any kind of hard cheese—from mozzarella to Colby.

Cheese will melt at "hot smoking" temperatures so you will need to use the cold smoking technique to produced smoked cheese. Brie can be smoked, but the trick is to smoke the entire wheel and not try to smoke cut pieces of the soft cheese.

Eggs

Smoked eggs probably aren't the first things that come to mind to make when you first purchase a smoker, but they're very easy to make. Some smokers simply put uncooked eggs on a rack in a smoker while meat is being smoked and a couple of hours later, the smoked eggs are ready. (Egg shells are permeable, so all the smoky flavor goes right in.)

Fish

Commercially smoked fish, particularly salmon, cod, trout, mackerel, and haddock, are readily available in most areas. If you want to smoke your own, head for a fishmonger to get the best price. Grocery chains like Ranch 99 have huge fish counters that include live crustaceans in tanks, and in cities along the coasts, you can often buy fish right off the boat.

Game

You've heard of "pulled pork" but have you ever eaten "pulled venison?" It's delicious. Venison is a perfect meat for the smoker, although it is lean and will need to be brined or it will dry out during cooking.

Elk is even leaner than venison, so experienced smokers pull out all the stops to ensure the meat stays moist—wrapping it in bacon, injecting it with broth, glazing it with sauce—whatever it takes.

If you don't know a hunter who'll share the bounty with you, Fossil Farms offers a full range of exotic and organic meats including buffalo, emu, ostrich, antelope, kangaroo (a red meat), and squab.

Another source of game meat is D'artagnan, which specializes in luxury edibles including caviar and truffles as well as cuts of meat ranging from buffalo steaks to wild boar.

Meat

Depending on what part of the country you're from, barbecue means beef (Texas) or pork (most of the South). But the United States is a nation of immigrants and as each new wave has entered the country, new customs and cuisines have also washed ashore. These days, smoked meat runs the gamut from rabbit (you'll need to wrap it in bacon) to ostrich (a hearty red meat). Or you could just stick to beef and pork.

What Cuts of Meat Make the Cut?

Smoking is a slow cooking process that can dry out tender, lean cuts of meat. Therefore, the best meat to use for smoking tends to be the fattier and tougher pieces, like beef brisket, pork shoulder, and beef and pork ribs. These cuts of meat (bonus) also tend to be cheaper than their leaner counterparts. Try these cuts to start:

Boston Butt—a cut of pork that weighs about 6-8 pounds. It's also simply called a "pork butt," even though it's cut from the pork shoulder, not lower down. It is commonly used to make "pulled pork."

Cadillac Cut (aka Hollywood Cut)—is a cut that saws the ribs all the way through rather than simply slicing them down the middle. The result of this cut is fewer but meatier ribs per rack. This is also known as the "Competition Cut."

Denver Ribs—is another term for lamb ribs, a tasty (but tough) alternative to a pricey rack of lamb or a boneless leg of lamb.

Picnic Roast-like the Boston Butt, this is a chunk of meat cut from the pork shoulder. It generally has less bone than the Boston Butt and also less marbling of fat.

You can get beef and pork in a huge variety of cuts almost anywhere, and in large urban areas, it's even possible to source really big hunks of meat of you need it. (A side of beef can weigh as much as 300 or more pounds.) Butchered and wrapped, that'll run you upwards of $1500, which is a whole lot of cheddar for a whole lot of meat. Still, if you're throwing a barbecue for a family reunion or a *quinceanera*, or a wedding and have a whole lot of people to feed, there are plenty of places that will provide you with grass-fed, hormone-free meat.

Online sources for beef:

Heritage Foods USA

Rain Crow Ranch

Getting Your Goat

Goat is a mainstay meat in Caribbean culture, where "jerk" and smoked goat are festive foods. In Hispanic cultures, smoked *cabrito* (kid goat) is a familiar dish. Goat is also eaten in Africa, Asia, and the Middle East. North America has been slow to acquire the taste (and adult goat *can* require a little getting used to), but now that foodies are leading the way, it's a lot easier to find sources for home smoking ventures.

Heritage Foods USA sells racks and legs of goat as well as different cuts of the animal, along with ground goat for your meat-patty needs. They also sell half-lambs and a selection of other meats, including poultry and waterfowl.

Poultry

Whole turkeys are available in almost any grocery store year 'round and increasingly, so are geese and ducks. At Thanksgiving and Christmas, some up-scale grocers also provide fresh and frozen game birds like pheasant and quail alongside the Rock Cornish game hens. For best results, always brine poultry of any kind before smoking, and that's especially necessary for game birds.

Recipes
POULTRY

Smoked Chicken Wings

These spicy chicken wings are sure to heat up any social gathering. Their spiciness makes them addicting, and will have people reaching for "just one more". They make for excellent appetizers during any social gathering.

Preparation Time: 20 minutes

Directions:

1. Be sure to coat all of your wings thoroughly with the rub ingredients. The best way to do this is to put all the ingredients in one bag. Shake the bag for a few minutes. This will coat the wings evenly.
2. Wings cook fast, so you only have to lay them out on the smoker for a little while before taking them out.
3. Serve them with your favorite dipping sauce.

Smoke Time: 1 hour

Smoke Temp: 325°

Ingredients:

5 lbs of chicken wings

3 tbsp. oil (olive, canola, or vegetable)

2 1/2 tbsp. black pepper

1 tsp. onion powder

1 tsp. garlic powder

1 tsp. seasoning salt

2 tsp. chili powder

2 tsp. red pepper flakes

Brine Smoked Chicken

During special occasions, you want a special main dish to honor the celebration. Once brined, the results are astounding for this chicken. The homey fragrance as it slowly smokes to perfection is sure to help set the mood for a wonderful evening.

Ingredients:

1 whole chicken

1 gallon of water (or enough to completely submerge your chicken)

3/4 cup salt

1 cup sugar

1 tbsp. of pepper

1 tbsp. of cayenne

Rub Recipe:

1/4 cup olive oil

1/4 cup soy sauce

2 tsp. onion powder

2 tsp. cayenne pepper

2 tsp. paprika

2 tsp. garlic powder or 2 crushed garlic cloves

1-1/2 tsp. black pepper

1 tbsp. dried oregano

1 tbsp. dried thyme

Serves: 6
Preparation Time: 15 minutes

Directions:

1. Boil water in a large pot. Add the salt and sugar so they dissolve in the water. Allow the water to cool down naturally, or add ice to it. After this, add the rest of the brine ingredients to the now cooled water.
2. Place the chicken in the brine water. Stick the whole pot into your fridge for ten hours.
3. Be sure to mix all your rub seasonings together. Use your hands to spread it evenly over your brined chicken and on the inside as well.
4. Place the chicken in the smoker, and allow to smoke for allotted time.

Smoke Time: 4 Hours

Smoke Temp: 250°

Smoked Chicken Legs

Chicken legs are a combination of the dark meat of drumsticks and thighs combined. When the dinner bell rings, it's fun to chow down on a crunchy chicken leg. Dig in to these simple, but enjoyable dinner staples.

Serves: 3
Preparation Time: 15 minutes

Directions:

1. Start your smoker up half an hour before you start cooking.
2. In a mixing bowl, stir together all the dry ingredients. Be sure to rub the olive oil all over the chicken legs.
3. Now rub the seasoning over the chicken legs until they're fully coated.
4. Place the chicken legs on the smoking rack.
5. Turn them over so they cook evenly. You may have to add more smoker chips as you do this.

Smoke Time: 2 Hours

Smoke Temp: 220°

Ingredients:

6 chicken legs

1 cup olive oil

1 tbsp. cayenne pepper

1 tbsp. paprika

2 tsp. salt

1 tbsp. onion powder

1 tbsp. dried thyme

1 tbsp. garlic powder

1 tbsp. pepper

Smoked Chicken Quarters

Chicken quarters may be a smaller cut, but they don't sacrifice on taste! These chicken quarters have a crispy, outer layer from the smoke curling along the skin. On the inside, the meat will peel away easily from the bone when you take that first bite.

Ingredients:

7-8 lb.s of chicken quarters (legs and thighs)

Water (to cover)

1 cup salt

1/2 cup sugar

1/4 cup olive oil

2 tsp. onion powder

2 tsp. cayenne pepper

2 tsp. paprika

2 tsp. garlic powder or 2 crushed garlic cloves

1-1/2 tsp. black pepper

1 tbsp. dried oregano

Serves: 10
Preparation Time: 10 minutes

Directions:

1. Brine your chicken quarters for six hours first. Boil up a pot of water and add in the sugar and salt. Once the water has cooled down, place the chicken in the pot. Place the pot in the fridge for six hours.
2. Mix the dry ingredients and oil together in a medium sized bowl.
3. Rub the olive oil on the chicken quarters. After this, add the seasoning mixture on to the chicken.
4. Lay the chicken on the smoking rack.

Be sure to check the inside temperature of your chicken is 165-170 degrees.

Smoke Time: 2 Hours

Smoke Temp: 220°

Thanksgiving Surprise

When Thanksgiving is here, knowing how to prepare a turkey is essential knowledge. Dazzle your guests this year with a magnificent centerpiece for the upcoming Thanksgiving holiday! This smoked turkey is easy to prepare and is very hearty and rich in flavor.

Serves: 12
Preparation Time: 10 minutes

Directions:

1. Rinse your turkey first. Dry it with some paper towels. In a bowl mix together the black pepper, savory, salt, and sage. Rub only half of the mixture on the inside of the turkey and the neck area. Be sure to loosen the skin of the turkey around the breast and legs. Rub the rest of the herb mixture underneath this loosened skin. After this, rub olive oil over the whole turkey.

A good rule of thumb for smoking turkey is to do it for 20 minutes for each lb. of turkey. Once done, remove the turkey from the smoker and serve.

Smoke Time: 4 Hours

Smoke Temp: 250°

Ingredients:

1 (12 lb.) thawed whole turkey, neck and giblets removed

1 tbsp. chopped fresh savory

1 tbsp. chopped fresh sage

1 tbsp. salt (optional)

1 tbsp. ground black pepper

1/8 cup olive oil

1/2 cup water

Honey Brined Turkey

Slide this honey-brined turkey into a smoker and get prepared for a tender and succulent meal. The smoky texture also flavors the meat so when you're left with those turkey leftovers, you're left with an inspiration to combine them in even more recipes.

Ingredients:

1 gallon hot water

1 lb. kosher salt

2 quarts vegetable broth

1 lb. honey

1 (7-lb.) bag of ice

1 (15 to 20-lb.) turkey, with giblets removed

Vegetable oil, for rubbing turkey

Serves: 12
Preparation Time: 15 minutes

Directions:

1. Heat up some water until it's warm. Place it in a large cooler. Add in the salt so it dissolves. Stir in the honey and vegetable brother. Add ice to the cooler and stir well. Put the turkey in the brine mixture. You want the breast to be facing upwards. Allow it to brine for twelve hours.
2. After the turkey is done brining, rub it down with vegetable oil.
3. Build a smoke bomb for your grill. Use heavy duty foil to wrap around some hickory wood chips.
4. Set your turkey in the smoker.
5. The turkey should be golden brown on its skin. If not, replace the wood chips. If the skin is golden, be sure to cover it in aluminum foil and allow it to keep cooking.
6. Once done, remove turkey from the smoker and serve.

Smoke Time: 1 Hour

Smoke Temp: 400°

Hickory Smoked Cornish Game Hen

When bringing home a game hen after a successful day of hunting, you want to enjoy your victory. Fire up the smoker and let the bird cook until its skin crackles and the pleasant aroma fills your backyard. A few mouths will start to water long before this meal is even finished smoking.

Serves: 4
Preparation Time: 10 minutes

Directions:

1. You're going to want to whisk together the pepper, salt, and dry rub in a small bowl. Spread the rub over the game hen. Place the hen on a tray, and cover it with some plastic wrap. Allow the hen to sit in the fridge for an hour.
2. Melt some butter in a pan over medium heat. Add your shallots and sauté them until they become tender. Be sure to season with pepper and salt. Add in the orange juice and chicken broth. Bring all of it to a simmer and allow it to reduce to ½ cup. Add the apple cider vinegar and hot sauce after about ten minutes. Be sure to taste test it first to check the seasoning is correct.
3. Place the game hen on the grill and cover it up. Smoke the hen for 40 minutes, and brush it with the glaze you made in a pan.
4. Be sure to get every inch of the hen as you can. Cover the hen up for another 15 minutes. Once you remove the hen from your smoker, cover it with foil for an additional 15 minutes before you serve it.

Smoke Time: 1 Hour

Smoke Temp: 275°

Ingredients:

1 tbsp. Neely's Dry Rub

1 tbsp. kosher salt, plus more for seasoning

1 tbsp. freshly ground black pepper, plus more for seasoning

4 (1 1/2 to 2 lb.s) Cornish game hens, washed and dried well

2 tsp. butter

1 shallot, finely chopped

1 cup chicken broth

3/4 cup freshly squeezed orange juice

2 tsp. apple cider vinegar

Dash of hot sauce

Award Winning Chicken Thighs

You're a winner, so you deserve to eat food that tastes like it! Once it's done tenderizing in the brine and has been slid into the smoker, these thighs come out nice and juicy. Enjoy these smoky chicken thighs in either a flamin' hot or smoky barbecue sauce.

Ingredients:

For Brine:

1 cup Water

1 cup Apple Juice

1 can of Sprite

1/2 C Kosher/Sea salt

1 T Pepper

For Chicken:

A package of Bone-in, Skin-on Chicken Thighs.

Basic Chicken Rub

Your favorite BBQ Sauce

Brine

Serves: 4
Preparation Time: 20 minutes

Directions:

1. Brine the chicken for up to several hours or half an hour at the least.
2. Be sure to rinse the chicken under some cool water. Place the skin side down. Dust the chicken rub onto the bottom of the chicken.
3. Place your chicken in the smoker.
4. Warm up your preferred bbq sauce in a small pan. You don't want the sauce to be too thick. If it is, thin it out with a little bit of Coke.
5. Dunk the chicken thighs into your pot of sauce after two hours in the smoker.
6. Allow the sauce to sit on the chicken for 15 minutes. Afterwards, allow them to cool down before eating.

Smoke Time: 2 Hours

Smoke Temp: 225°

Chicken Breast

Chicken breasts are a favorite among many people. These chicken breasts are guaranteed to have a bit of a kick with them. Combined with a sweet barbeque sauce, they're sure to please.

Serves: 10
Preparation Time: 15 minutes

Directions:

1. Be sure to mix all your chicken seasonings together in one large bowl. You'll also want to make sure you have plenty of barbecue sauce to coat each of your chicken breasts.
2. Coat all of your chicken breasts with the seasoning and barbecue sauce.
3. Flip the breast over halfway through smoking. The internal temperature of the meat should reach at least 160 degrees.
4. Allow the breasts to cool down before you serve them.

Smoke Time: 1 Hour & 15 Mins

Smoke Temp: 250°

Ingredients:

10 individual chicken breasts or a 5 lb. bag of chicken breasts

2 tsp. salt

2 tsp. paprika

2 tsp. garlic powder

2 tsp. garlic salt

2 tsp. black pepper

1/2 tbsp. cayenne pepper

1 tbsp. dried thyme

1 tbsp. dried oregano

4 tsp. brown sugar

1 bottle sweet barbecue sauce

Applewood Smoked Chicken

This chicken has a combination of hot and spicy mixed in with a hint of sweetness. The skin will come out crispy with that smoky flavor to meld all the flavors together into a tantalizing experience for your taste buds.

Enjoy the wonderful aroma of this chicken once you've taken it out of the smoker, because you're in for a treat.

Ingredients:

1 tbsp. salt

1 tbsp. paprika

1 tbsp. garlic powder

1 tbsp. garlic salt

1 tbsp. black pepper

1 tbsp. crushed red pepper flakes

1/4 tbsp. cayenne pepper

1/2 tbsp. dried thyme

1/2 tbsp. dried oregano

2 tsp. brown sugar

1 whole chicken, halved

Serves: 2
Preparation Time: 10 minutes

Directions:

1. Get out a medium bowl and mix together all your dry ingredients. Rub your seasoning all over your chicken. After this, cover your chicken up in some plastic wrap. Store in the fridge for one hour.
2. Put the chicken on the grill.
3. Once done, serve as the main dish.

Smoke Time: 1 Hour

Smoke Temp: 250°

Bacon Wrapped Chicken Breasts

Ah, yes! Everyone knows about America's obsession with bacon. Feast on these bacon-wrapped chicken breasts as the bacon forms into a rich, crispy coating on the outside. The flavor of the bacon and smoke will soak into the chicken breasts, and this will give that extra flair of flavor to make this a dish to remember.

Serves: 4
Preparation Time: 10 minutes

Directions:

1. Brine the chicken with the brine ingredients. Allow them to brine for two hours in the fridge. You may want to flip the breasts over an hour in just to make sure they are all soaked evenly.
2. Rinse the chicken breasts, and cover them with the rub you made.
3. Lay down three pieces of bacon down on a cutting board or other clean area. Lay one chicken breast on top of the bacon.
4. Roll the chicken breast over so the bacon wraps around it. Use the toothpicks to hold the bacon onto the chicken.
5. Place the chicken breasts in the smoker. Space them about one inch apart so the smoke can get all sides.
6. Half an hour after the breasts are done cooking, brush the top of them with a light coat of your smoky barbecue sauce.
7. The internal temperature should be 165 degrees before serving the chicken.

Smoke Time: 3 Hours

Smoke Temp: 230°

Ingredients:

For the brine:

4 cups of cold drinking water

1/4 cup kosher salt

1/4 cup brown sugar

For the chicken:

4 -6 chicken breasts (boneless and skinless)

toothpick

regular cut bacon (3 slices per breast)

ribs or chicken, rub

smoky barbecue sauce

AsparagusStuffedSmokedChickenBreasts

Now you can enjoy the strong vegetable taste of asparagus hidden right in your meat! Let the juices mix and marry each other. Just wrap the chicken around the asparagus, and you're ready to go!

Ingredients:

4-6 boneless, skinless chicken breasts

Your choice of rub

8-12 stalks of asparagus (the thinner stalks are more tender)

4-6 slices of bacon (thin sliced seems to crisp up better in the smoker)

Toothpicks (optional)

Serves: 10
Preparation Time: 15 minutes

Directions:

1. Apply the rub to the chicken. Allow them to sit in the fridge overnight.
2. Lay the chicken down on a cutting board. Place a piece of asparagus on top, and roll the chicken over the asparagus. Use toothpicks to keep the asparagus in place.
3. Once you've done that, wrap some bacon over the middle of the chicken. Secured it with another toothpick.
4. Sprinkle some rub on top of the "stuffed" chicken with the asparagus and bacon on it.
5. Cover up the chicken and place in the fridge for 4 hours. Overnight if you want that extra flavor.
6. Allow the chicken to cook in the smoker. Allow it to cool for a few minutes before serving.

Smoke Time: 1 Hour, 20 Mins

Smoke Temp: 225°

Smoked Turkey Legs

Turkey legs are massive. Once they're smoked, dripping with barbecue sauce, and on your plate it's hard to resist digging in. They have enough meat on their bones to satisfy even the hungriest of carnivores. An excellent dish to enjoy at Disneyland, now you can have them at home too!

Serves: 6
Preparation Time: 30 minutes

Directions:

1. Loosen the skin of the turkey legs beforehand. You can do this by running your fingers under it. Try to go as far as possible, being careful not to tear it.
2. Mix together the oil and Worcestershire sauce. Rub the mixture over the turkey legs. Be sure to get some of it under the skin. Next, sprinkle the rub over the legs.
3. Put the legs in a plastic bag. Store in the fridge.
4. Take out the turkey legs from the fridge. Allow them to sit out for half an hour so they come up to room temperature.
5. Warm up the mop mixture.
6. Place the turkey legs in the smoker. Be sure to mop the legs every 45 minutes.
7. Once the turkey legs are done, serve them hot. They're best eaten with your fingers with some barbeque sauce.

Smoke Time: 4 Hours

Smoke Temp: 220°

Ingredients:

6 turkey legs

3 tsp. Worcestershire sauce

1 tbsp. vegetable oil

Dry Rub, recipe follows

Mop, recipe follows

Sweet & Spicy BBQ sauce

Dry Rub:

1/4 cup chipotle seasoning, (recommended: North of the Border Chipotle Seasoning)

1 to 2 tsp. mild dried ground red chili or paprika

1 tbsp. packed brown sugar

Mop Mixture:

1 cup white vinegar

1 tbsp. BBQ Sauce, (recommended: North of the Border Chipotle Barbecue Sauce)

1 tbsp. vegetable oil

Sweet and Spicy Chicken Wings

When it comes to eating chicken wings, spicy tends to be a favorite at any social gathering. So if you're looking for an addition to set off the spice, toss some sweet flavoring in there. You may feel a burning sensation on your tongue, but you'll be reaching for these wings again and again.

Ingredients:

2 1/2 tsp. ground black pepper

1 tbsp. onion powder

1 tbsp. chili powder

1 tbsp. garlic powder

1 tbsp. seasoned salt

5 lb.s chicken wings, rinsed and dried

1 cup mL honey

1/2 cup hot barbecue sauce (or more to taste; use your favorite and the hottest sauce you can stand)

3 tsp. apple juice

Serves: 6
Preparation Time: 20 minutes

Directions:

1. Sift together the garlic powder, onion powder, pepper, and chili powder.
2. Put all of the chicken wings in a large zippered plastic bag. Pour the dry rub into the bag, and shake everything together. Allow the rub to sit on the wings for half an hour or overnight.
3. Put your wings in the grate. You want them to cook with indirect heat.
4. Mix the barbecue sauce, apple juice, and honey altogether in a saucepan. Cook all of it over medium heat until it's been warmed through.
5. Put the wings in a disposable pan. Pour the now warm sauce over the wings, and coat them evenly. Toss them a bit if you have to. Cover and smoke the wings for another half hour. Stir them every couple of minutes. Once they're finished, allow them to cool for a few minutes before serving.

Smoke Time: 50 Mins

Smoke Temp: 225°

PORK

Smoked Pork Ribs

Pork ribs are known for having a large amount of meat on them compared to beef ribs. These ones have a bit of a kick to them. It's offset by the smoky flavor soaking into them. When they're done smoking, the meat will be separating from the bone with just a small tug of the fingers.

Ingredients:

Rub:

1/4 cup ancho chili powder

2 tsp. Spanish paprika

2 tsp. freshly ground black pepper

2 tsp. dry mustard

2 tsp. kosher salt

2 tsp. ground coriander

1 tbsp. dried oregano

1 tbsp. ground cumin

2 tsp. chile de arbol

2 racks St. Louis-style pork ribs, 12 ribs each, membrane removed

1/4 cup canola oil

Mop Mixture:

2 cups cider vinegar

2 tsp. light brown sugar

1/2 tbsp. cayenne powder

Few dashes hot pepper sauce (recommended: Tabasco)

1 tbsp. kosher salt

1/4 tbsp. freshly ground black pepper

1 quart apple cider

Smoke Flavored BBQ Sauce

Serves: 4
Preparation Time: 30 minutes

Directions:

1. Get a small bowl, and combine all the spices inside it. Brush each side of all the racks with a little bit of oil and your spice mixture. Wrap it all up in plastic and refrigerate overnight, for 12 hours.
2. Get a large pot heated up over low heat. Add all the mop ingredients into it. You're going to want to bring it all to a simmer, and just cook it until the sugar has completely dissolved. Allow it cool at room temperature.
3. Take the rips out of the fridge one hour before it's time to start smoking them. Also, at this time put your apple cider in a heatproof pan and place it within the smoker.
4. Place your ribs on the rack in the smoker. Once every hour for the first five hours you're going to brush your ribs with the mop. On the last hour, brush your ribs with the barbecue sauce every 10 minutes.
5. Afterwards, take your ribs off the smoking rack and serve.

Smoke Time: 6 Hours

Smoke Temp: 220°

Apple-Injected Smoked Pork

This recipe uses Applewood chips to give the pork a smoky flavoring inside and out. Instead of letting the marinade absorb into the meat, it's injected directly into it. The meat becomes tender and starts falling apart once it's done smoking.

Serves: 12
Preparation Time: 10 minutes

Directions:

1. Get a large bowl, and whisk together all ingredients for your marinade.
2. Place your pork in a large casserole dish. Use a syringe to inject your marinade ¾ of the way inside of the pork. You're going to want to do this several times in a different place each time on your eat.
3. Cover the pork in plastic wrap and store in the fridge between 4-12 hours.
4. Place pork in the smoker.
5. Drain off any liquid that has remained on the meat, and be sure to pat it dry. Season the pork with your dry rub seasoning so it has a better taste. You're going to want to cover both sides.
6. Allow the pork to cool for a few minutes before serving.

Smoke Time: 6 Hours

Smoke Temp: 275°

Ingredients:

2 cups apple cider

2 tsp. dry rub seasoning

2 tsp. apple cider vinegar

2 tsp. honey

1/2 tbsp. cayenne pepper

1/4 cup orange juice

1/2 cup lemon juice

Dash Worcestershire sauce

2 tsp. kosher salt

1 (6 to 8-lb.) pork butt

Smoked Pork Chops

These pork chops are tender with just a hint of sweetness. They'll melt in your mouth as soon as you sink your teeth in them. Dripping with spices blended together in perfect harmony, this will be a welcome addition to any dinner table.

Ingredients:

4 tbsp. salt

2 tsp. freshly ground black pepper

2 tsp. dark brown sugar

2 tsp. ground thyme

2 tsp. onion powder

1 tbsp. cayenne pepper

4 center cut, bone-in pork chops

Buttermilk BBQ Sauce:

1 cup apple cider

1 tbsp. brown sugar

1/2 preferred BBQ sauce

1 tbsp. buttermilk

Serves: 4
Preparation Time: 15 minutes

Directions:

1. In a small bowl mix together cayenne pepper, salt, onion powder, black pepper, thyme, and brown sugar. After this you're going to want to rub your pork chops with this mixture. Wrap the chops in plastic wrap and store in the fridge for four hours.
2. Place your chops in the smoker.
3. Get a medium saucepan and heat it up to medium-low heat. Add in the brown sugar and apple cider. Stir everything together. You're going to let the mixture reduce for only 25 minutes. Turn the heat down to low, and pour in your preferred barbecue sauce. Stir everything well.
4. Once the sauce has been thoroughly warmed, turn off the heat source. Add in the buttermilk and stir it all together. Serve this over the pork chops, and you're done!

Smoke Time: 1 Hour 10 Mins

Smoke Temp: 275°

Smoked Boston Butt Roast

On its own, a Boston butt roast tastes amazing. Add in the handmade seasoning, a few bay leaves, and a few more choice spices and you've got a delicacy on your hands. Guests will be eager to tear into this smoked roast once it's been cooked and served.

Serves: 6
Preparation Time: 20 minutes

Directions:

1. On one side of your roast sprinkle two tsp. of the House Seasoning. Be sure to rub it in well with your fingers. Flip your roast over and rub in the remaining two tsp. of the House Seasoning. Repeat this process with your seasoned salt.
2. Place your roast on a large pan for roasting. Add in the bay leaves, onion, and water. Place the roast in your smoker.
3. The internal temperature for the roast should be 170 degrees. Once it is, allow it to cool for a few minutes.

Serve this roast with sweet or smoky BBQ sauce.

Smoke Time: 4 Hours

Smoke Temp: 350°

Ingredients:

1 (5 lb) pork butt roast

4 tsp. House Seasoning, recipe follows

2 tsp. seasoned salt

1 medium onion, sliced

1 cup water

3 bay leaves

Sweet or Smoky BBQ sauce

House Seasoning:

1 cup salt

1/4 cup black pepper

1/4 cup garlic powder

Sweet BBQ Pork Shoulder

Getting pork to cook just right can be a bit of a challenge at first. While still excellent, this is an easier way to prepare pork shoulder. There is no hassle, and best of all it retains that tasty aroma to it when it starts to sizzle and cook.

Ingredients:

1 (5-6 lb.) pork shoulder or Boston butt pork roast

2 tsp. salt

Sweet BBQ Sauce

Serves: 6
Preparation Time:

Directions:

1. Sprinkle the salt over your pork shoulder. Cover it up and chill it in the fridge for half an hour.
2. Place the pork inside the smoker directly in the center. Cover it up and leave your ventilation holes open on the smoker.
3. Allow the meat to cook for five and a half hours. The internal temperature of your pork should be 165 degrees. Turn the pork over for the last two hours of its smoking.
4. Once you've removed the pork, give it a few minutes to cool. Chop it up and serve with sweet BBQ sauce.

Smoke Time: 5 ½ Hours

Smoke Temp: 250°

Smoked Pork Sausage

Being able to make your own sausages is very convenient. You know exactly what's going into the sausage, and can make it to your personal preferences. Feel free to experiment with this recipe, and add to it to suit your own unique tastes.

Serves: 30
Preparation Time: 60 minutes

Directions:

1. Cut all of the meat into cubes. Mix them all together in an extra-large bowl with the spices.
2. Using a sausage grinder, pass this mixed meat and spices through a medium plate on the grinder.
3. Stuff your sausages in natural pork casings so you'll be able to smoke them.
4. Place them in the smoker.
5. You may have to switch out the sausages to smoke them. You can adjust how many you're making by using less meat and spices.

Smoke Time: 3 Hours

Smoke Temp: 230°

Ingredients:

20 lbs of home-dressed lean pork meat

10 lbs of clear fat pork

1/2 lb fine salt (best quality)

2 tsp. sugar

1 tbsp. ginger

2 tsp. pepper

1 tbsp. sage

2 tsp. cure (either Instacure #1 or Prague Powder #1)

Sweet Smoked Pork Ribs

This is a great beginner recipe for all the rib lovers out there. Once they're done, steam will be rising off the back of these babies. Once you start eating them they're practically falling off the bone!

Ingredients:

1/4 cup salt

1/4 cup white sugar

2 tsp. packed brown sugar

2 tsp. ground black pepper

2 tsp. ground white pepper

2 tsp. onion powder

1 tbsp. garlic powder

1 tbsp. chili powder

1 tbsp. paprika

1 tbsp. ground cumin

10 lbs baby back pork ribs

1 cup apple juice

1/4 cup packed brown sugar

1/4 cup sweet BBQ sauce

Serves: 15
Preparation Time: 20 minutes

Directions:

1. In small bowl combine salt, cumin, white sugar, paprika, 2 tsp. of brown sugar, chili powder, black pepper, garlic powder, white pepper, and onion powder. Rub this mixture onto the back of the rips on all of the sides. Wrap your ribs in plastic wrap. Store in the fridge for half an hour.
2. Start your smoker. Put your ribs on the rack.
3. In a small bowl combine barbeque sauce, apple juice, and ¼ brown sugar. Every 30 to 45 minutes brush the ribs with the barbeque sauce for the first hour. Brush the sauce onto the rips during its last half hour of cooking.
4. When the ribs have finished, wrap them up in aluminum foil. Allow them to sit for an additional 15 minutes. You may serve them afterward.

Smoke Time: 4 Hours

Smoke Temp: 270°

Smoked Pork Loin

Pork loin is a melt in your mouth meat. It's like a candy you savor as it slowly dissolves, leaving you to reach for another bite to eat. It goes great alongside a few steamed vegetables.

Serves: 10
Preparation Time: 10 minutes

Directions:

1. Trim off the silver skin (white stuff. off your pork loin. Coat the loin with some olive oil. Sprinkle your rub on each side of your loin.
2. Put the loin on the smoker. Internal temperature of the loin should be 150 degrees.
3. Afterwards, wrap the loin in aluminum foil. Do this lightly.
4. Preheat the broiler.
5. Put your jam in a medium sized bowl and add 1/3 of your chipotle sauce. Mix everything together and taste to make sure it's to your preference.
6. Cover the loin with glaze. Place it in the broiler pan and allow it to cook in there for only three minutes.
7. Once it's done, cut the pork going against the grain, and serve.

Ingredients:

1 (4-lb.) pork loin

Extra-virgin olive oil, as needed

3 tsp. dry spice rub for pork

1 (10-ounce) jar seedless raspberry jam

1 (5-ounce) bottle chipotle hot pepper sauce (recommended: Tabasco)

Smoke Time: 2 Hours

Smoke Temp: 230°

Smoked Pork Tenderloin

Tenderloin is best described as a soft meat. It's one of the best cuts of pork you can ever try. Once it's been smoked, and slowly heated up all the flavorings will balance in a perfect melody for your taste buds to enjoy.

Ingredients:

1 or 2 pork tenderloins (1.5-2 lb.s each)

½ cup marinade

½ cup sweet BBQ sauce

Serves: 4
Preparation Time: 15 minutes

Directions:

1. Place your pork loin in your chosen marinade. Allow it to sit in the marinade for 3 hours or overnight if you have the time.
2. Drain the marinade. Place your pork loin on the rack.
3. Half an hour before taking the loin out of the smoker, baste it with barbeque sauce.
4. Remove from the smoker once the pork loin is done smoking. Wrap the pork loin in some foil for ten minutes.
5. Slice the pork loin thinly. Serve with sweet BBQ sauce on the side.

Smoke Time: 3 Hours

Smoke Temp: 225°

German Pork Hock

Pork hock doesn't give enough love. It's inexpensive, but that doesn't mean it can't have taste delicious. Use just a few simple vegetables for flavoring, a dash of salt, and you'll be pleasantly surprised by this new experience in pork hock cuisine.

Serves: 2
Preparation Time: 20 minutes

Directions:

1. Put your hocks, vegetables, 1 tbsp. salt, and 1 tbsp. peppercorns I a pot. Add in some water and bring it all to a boil. Reduce the heat and allow it to simmer for 3 hours. Be careful not to overcook the hocks.
2. Drain the hocks and vegetables. In a baking dish or pan add in your hocks, vegetables, and only a small amount of cooking oil.
3. Smoke the pork hocks.
4. Recommended you serve this dish with sauerkraut and potatoes.

Smoke Time: 1 ½ Hours

Smoke Temp: 250°

Ingredients:

1 leek, well cleaned, diced

1 stalk celery, diced

1 carrot, diced

1 onion, diced

1 - 2 meaty pork hocks

salt, peppercorns, cumin (if desired)

Asian Honey Pork Chops

These Asian inspired pork chops are sure to please lovers of Asian cuisine all around. The sesame seed oil gives them a succulent edge you won't find in many other dishes. Honey soaks into meat allowing it to come out so soft, it will melt on the tongue.

Ingredients:

2-4 pork chops, 1/2 inch to 3/4 inch thick

1 tbsp toasted sesame seed oil or olive oil

1/2 cup chicken broth

1/2 cup honey

1/4 cup soy sauce

2 tsp. ketchup

1/4 tbsp. crushed red pepper flakes

1/4 tbsp. garlic salt

Serves: 8
Preparation Time: 10 minutes

Directions:

1. Sprinkle your chops with oil and garlic salt.
2. Place the chops in a greased pan. Mix the rest of the remaining ingredients, and pour these over the chops.
3. Smoke your chops. Save the extra sauce for some rice on the side.

Smoke Time: 2 Hours

Smoke Temp: 275°

Pit Smoked Pork Shoulder

Looking to prepare some pulled pork for an up and coming barbecue? Smoke the pork shoulder first to give it that extra addition of taste. The pork will come out tender and easier to shred.

Serves: 6
Preparation Time: 20 minutes

Directions:

1. Mix all of your spices together in a small bowl.
2. In a medium sized bowl, whisk together your ingredients for the injector. You want the salt and sugar to be completely dissolved.
3. Take your roasts out of the fridge.
4. Inject both roasts with your liquid.
5. Pat your roasts with the dry rub you made. Allow the roasts to sit for one and a half hours.
6. Place pork roasts in the smoker.
7. Once they're done, shred finely to make pulled pork.

Smoke Time: 12 Hours

Smoke Temp: 225°

Ingredients:

2 pork shoulder, roasts

Shoulder Rub:

1/4 cup brown sugar

1/2 cup white sugar

1/2 cup paprika

1/3 cup garlic powder

2 tsp. white salt

1 tbsp. chili powder

1 tbsp. cayenne pepper

2 tsp. black pepper

1 tbsp. dried oregano

1 tbsp. cumin

Injection Liquid:

3/4 cup apple juice

1/2 cup water

1/2 cup sugar

3 tsp. salt

2 tsp. Worcestershire sauce

Slow Smoked Pork Ribs

These ribs take a little more time to smoke. However, for your patience you're rewarded with ribs that are practically falling off the bone once you serve them. Add in spicy BBQ sauce, some grilled corn, and you're all set for a party.

Ingredients:

8 lbs pork loin baby back ribs

1/4 cup yellow honey mustard

1/4 cup brown sugar

1/3 cup paprika

1/4 cup onion powder

1/4 cup granulated garlic powder

2 tsp. dried parsley flakes

1 -2 tbsp. chipotle chili pepper flakes

1 tbsp. black pepper

2 tsp. chili powder

1 tbsp. ground cumin

1 tbsp. salt

Spicy BBQ sauce

Serves: 8
Preparation Time: 20 minutes

Directions:

1. Bring your ribs up to room temperature.
2. Mix all the rub ingredients together.
3. Rub this mustard mixture over every surface of your ribs.
4. Place your ribs on the smoker. When their halfway done wrap them up in heavy duty foil. Smoke for the remaining time.
5. Un-wrap the ribs for one hour afterward.
6. You can eat these ribs with spicy BBQ sauce.

Smoke Time: 4 Hours

Smoke Temp: 200°

Spice-Roasted Pork Tenderloin

This pork tenderloin is just a little spicier than some other recipes. Combine that with a paprika sprinkled on top to give it an extra flair, and you're guaranteed to have pork tenderloin sizzling with flavor. Feast your senses on this pork tenderloin with some grilled asparagus and mashed potatoes.

Serves: 8
Preparation Time: 10 minutes

Directions:

1. Place your tenderloins on a baking sheet.
2. Get a small bowl and mix together the cinnamon, paprika, oregano, cumin, and garlic powder.
3. Rub olive oil over the tenderloin. Be sure to season it with salt and pepper.
4. Sprinkle your spice mix over the entire tenderloin.
5. Place tenderloins in the smoker. Once done serve them with one or two sides.

Smoke Time: 1 Hour

Smoke Temp: 275°

Ingredients:

4 pork tenderloins (about 4 lbs.)

2 tsp. smoked paprika (pimenton)

2 tsp. ground cumin

1 tbsp. garlic powder

1 tbsp. dried oregano

1/2 tbsp. cinnamon

2 tsp. extra-virgin olive oil

Kosher salt and freshly ground pepper

Fish & Seafood

Smoked Salmon

Salmon is a fish that everyone raves about. If you're a beginner in the smoked salmon department this recipe is a good place to start. It's easy and simple, but the spices and sugar blend together in perfect harmony for this delicacy.

Serves: 4
Preparation Time: 10 minutes

Ingredients:

1 salmon fillet (about 2 lb.s)

2 tsp. brown sugar

2 tsp. salt

1/2 tbsp. pepper

Directions:

1. Sprinkle your salmon with some pepper, brown sugar, and salt. Cover and refrigerate it for four hours.
2. Place salmon in the smoker. Allow the salmon to cool to room temperature.
3. Store the salmon in the fridge overnight. Or eat while still warm.

Smoke Time: 1 ½ Hours

Smoke Temp: 250°

Smoked Catfish

After a day of fishing you may have a few extra catfish lying around. Why not toss them in the smoker? All you need is some salt, cold water, black pepper, and you're good to go for serving these up for lunch or dinner.

Ingredients:

2 lbs of catfish fillets

1 quart of cold water

1 cup non-iodized salt

Coarse black pepper

Serves: 4
Preparation Time: 10 minutes

Directions:

1. Stir salt and water together until the salt has dissolved. Place the fillets in a freezer safe bag. Add in the brine you just made, and place the fillets in the fridge for an hour.
2. Take the catfish fillets out of the bag and give them a rinse. Be sure to pat them dry.
3. Add coarse black pepper to each side of the fillets. Press your black pepper into the fish so it won't fall off while smoking.
4. Smoke the catfish.
5. Once the flesh begins to flake, the fish is done.

Smoke Time: 1 Hour

Smoke Temp: 225°

Smoked Shrimp

Shrimp is one of those finger foods that can make you want to smack your lips. These babies have just a hint of garlic on them, some butter, and even olive oil to make them extra tender. They'll melt on your tongue like candies once they're done smoking.

Serves: 2
Preparation Time: 10 minutes

Directions:

1. In a large bowl mix the shrimp with the pepper, salt, and olive oil. Toss if you have to.
2. Lay your shrimp down in one layer to smoke.
3. While the shrimp is smoking, mix together the salt, herbs, butter, and garlic for taste. Drizzle this over the cooked shrimp. Serve any remaining garlic herb butter as an additional dipping sauce.

Smoke Time: 20 Mins

Smoke Temp: 225°

Ingredients:

1 lb. shrimp, deveined

1 tbsp. garlic infused olive oil

salt and pepper to taste

¼ cup grass-fed ghee or butter, melted

1 clove garlic, minced

1 tbsp. fresh basil and/or parsley, minced

Smoked Tuna

This smoked tuna will melt in your mouth after you sink your teeth into it. The meat is very soft, and sure to please even the pickiest of palates. Eat these alongside some steamed vegetables for an excellent meal.

Ingredients:

4 (10-oz.) tuna steaks

2 quarts water

2/3 cup coarse kosher salt

1/2 cup firmly packed brown sugar

5 bay leaves, crumbled

2 tsp. fresh lemon juice

Vegetable oil

2 tsp. coarsely ground black peppercorns

4 cups dry white wine

Serves: 4
Preparation Time: 15 minutes

Directions:

1. Put the tuna steaks in a zip lock bag, preferably a heavy duty one. Mix together water, salt, brown sugar, bay leaves, and lemon juice. Pour this over the tuna steaks. Zip the bag up and store in the fridge for 3 hours. Turn the bag over every half hour.
2. Take the tuna steaks out of the brine. Rinse them and pat them dry. Allow them to sit on an air rack for half an hour. Brush each side of the tuna steaks with vegetable oil. Also, pat a little bit of pepper onto the fillets as well.
3. Place your tuna steaks inside the smoker and close the lid.
4. Once the tuna is done, serve with some choice sides.

Smoke Time: 3 Hours

Smoke Temp: 225°

Smoked Tilapia

Tilapia is a crowd pleaser. No wonder, it's a great fish to eat! Smoking tilapia may seem unusual, don't let that stop you. As its smoking, the flesh of tilapia will begin to flake. This gives it a crispy exterior while keeping the main meat of the fish soft and juicy.

Serves: 5
Preparation Time: 15 minutes

Directions:

1. In a small bowl mix together your olive oil, black pepper, herb seasoning, salt, garlic, and basil. Rub this mixture into your tilapia on each side.
2. Place your tilapia in the smoker.
3. When the tilapia is done cooking, serve it with a slice of lemon or squeeze the lemon over it.

Smoke Time: 2 Hours

Smoke Temp: 250°

Ingredients:

5 tilapia fillets

Ground black pepper to taste

Salt to taste

2 tsp. chopped fresh dill or basil

3 tsp. garlic and herb seasoning

1 tbsp. olive oil

1 lemon, sliced

Smoked Cod

Did you catch some cod while fishing? Smoke your fine prize to celebrate your awesome catch. The meat will develop a flaky texture, giving the fillet a small hint of a crunch when you bite into it. There is a hint of spice tossed in for that nice little flair of flavor.

Ingredients:

4 to 5 fresh cod fillets

2 gallons water

2 cups orange juice

4 cloves garlic, crushed

4 tbsp. pepper

1 tbsp. onion powder

Kosher salt

1 cup paprika

2 tbsp. cayenne

Serves: 2
Preparation Time: 15 minutes

Directions:

1. Lay the cod out on a few paper towels. Sprinkle your fish with some salt. Wait half and hour, and then rinse the cod off under some cold water.
2. Mix the brine mixture in one gallon of water, 2 tsp. of pepper and garlic, orange juice, ½ cup paprika, and ¼ cup salt. Allow the fish to soak in the brine for 45 minutes.
3. Mix the paprika, cayenne, onion powder, and remaining pepper in a small bowl. Rub this mixture into the cod on both sides. Rub it in as best you can. If the cod has skin on it, only rub the spices where the meat is exposed.
4. Place cod in the smoker.
5. Once done allow it to cool for a few minutes before serving.

Smoke Time: 2 Hours

Smoke Temp: 250°

Smoked King Crab Legs

Crab legs are soft, tender, and a delicacy. Once they've been smoked they taste even more amazing. You just need a few simple ingredients to have the best smoked crab legs anyone has ever tasted. When these crab legs are done the meat will come out white and juicy!

Serves: 2
Preparation Time: 10 minutes

Directions:

1. Stir together the grated lemon rind, butter, salt, parsley, and lemon juice all together. Crack the crab legs open and brush with the butter mixture.
2. Be sure to coat the rack of your smoker with cooking spray.
3. Smoke the crab legs. Once done eat with a side of melted butter for dipping.

Smoke Time: 20 minutes

Smoke Temp: 225°

Ingredients:

1 cup butter or margarine, melted

1/4 cup fresh lemon juice

1 tbsp. minced fresh parsley

1/2 tbsp. grated lemon rind

Pinch salt

5 lb.s frozen king crab legs, thawed

Smoked Lobster Tails

Lobster tails are a tender treat to have. Reward yourself with some lobster tails for being so awesome. Just brush a little butter on top with the steam rolling off of them, and then dig in.

Ingredients:

1 cup butter or margarine, melted

1/4 cup fresh lemon juice

1 tbsp. minced fresh parsley

1/2 tbsp. grated lemon rind

Pinch salt

4 frozen lobster tails, thawed (about 2 lb.s)

Serves: 2
Preparation Time: 10 minutes

Directions:

1. Mix together the salt, butter, lemon juice, parsley, and lemon rind. Brush this over the lobster tails.
2. Place the lobster tails in the smoker.
3. The flesh should be white and firm once done.

Smoke Time: 1 Hour

Smoke Temp: 225°

Smoked Clams

Clams are very convenient to eat. They come in their own little packages, and most of the time you don't have to do much to prepare them. All you need is some garlic, butter, and beer to make a feast of these little guys. Little puffs of steam will be rolling off of them once they pop open, and are ready to eat.

Serves: 4
Preparation Time: 10 minutes

Directions:

1. Soak the all the clams in some water for two hours. Be sure to scrub the clams as well under some cold water after soaking them.
2. Mince the butter, garlic, and one twelve ounce beer. Arrange the clams on a metal tray. Add this mixture to the tray.
3. Place the tray inside the smoker. Cook your clams for only 20 minutes in the smoker, or until they have opened.
4. Once the clams are done, add in your preferred sauce and serve.

Smoke Time: 20 Mins

Smoke Temp: 200°

Ingredients:

36 fresh clams

5 cloves of garlic

4 tbsp. of butter

Beer

Smoked Snow Crab Legs

Snow Crab Legs are soft and juicy. When they're smoked, the meat turns white becomes succulent. Dip these crab legs into some butter so they're even more supple when you enjoy them.

Ingredients:

3-5 lb.s of snow crab legs

1 cup of butter

1/4 cup lemon juice

2 tsp. lemon pepper seasoning

2 tsp. garlic powder or minced garlic

Serves: 3
Preparation Time: 15 minutes

Directions:

1. Put the garlic, butter, lemon pepper seasoning, and lemon juice in a small mixing bowl. Mix everything together and microwave it for only 30 seconds. Stir it all together.
2. Place the crab legs in the smoker. Baste them with the mixture you just made once every 10 minutes.
3. Once the snow crab legs are done, take them out of the smoker. Either eat with some butter to dip them into or eat the meat as is.

Smoke Time: 25 Mins

Smoke Temp: 225°

Smoked Scallops

Scallops are notorious for being one of those foods you can't get enough of. When you smoke these scallops, they will pop open with quiet little sizzle. It's fast, easy, and above all they come out creamy and delicious.

Serves: 4
Preparation Time: 15 minutes

Directions:

1. Mix together the sugar, water, and salt together in a bowl. Do this until all the sugar and salt has dissolved. Rinse your scallops off thoroughly before placing them in the brine. Cover it up and chill them for one hour. Drain afterward.
2. Place the scallops in one layer on a wire rack. Chill them for another hour.
3. You will want to place a water pan in the smoker. Add water only up to the fill line.
4. Be sure to wrap your strips of prosciutto around each scallop. Secure them with wooden picks. Put all the scallops on an upper rack in the smoker. Sprinkle the green onions onto your scallops. Don't worry if most fall into the water.
5. Once done serve the scallops up.

Smoke Time: 20 Mins

Smoke Temp: 225°

Ingredients:

6 cups water

1/3 cup kosher salt

1/4 cup sugar

36 sea scallops

2/3 lb. thinly sliced prosciutto

6 green onions, sliced

Bacon Wrapped Smoked Scallops

Still craving scallops? Wrap them up in some bacon, and listen to them sizzle in the smoker! The juices of these two will meld perfectly to create a dish that's sure to amaze.

Ingredients:

1 dozen sea scallops

¼ cup Olive oil

1 tbsp. Preferred rub

1 lb of thin sliced bacon

Serves: 1
Preparation Time: 15 minutes

Directions:

1. Place the scallops in a zip lock bag. Add in the olive oil, and roll it around to coat your scallops evenly in the oil.
2. Toss the rub in, and seal the bag again. Roll it around so the scallops are now coated in the rub.
3. Let the scallops sit in the fridge with the bag to marinate for one hour.
4. Take the scallops out of the bag and roll them up in the bacon.
5. Use a toothpick to keep the bacon in place on the scallops.
6. Arrange the scallops on the grate of the smoker.

Once the scallops are finished smoking serve and enjoy.

Smoke Time: 45 Mins

Smoke Temp: 220°

Apple Smoked Striped Bass

When you have a prize winning bass on your hands, you need a way to prepare it to honor the occasion. Just place your catch in the smoker, and watch it light up. Enjoy it with the spicy flair of a few habanero chilies. Garnish the bass with a little bit of lemon squeezed on top for additional flavor.

Serves: 2
Preparation Time: 15 minutes

Directions:

1. Put your chilies in a coffee grinder. You want to do this so they're finally ground up. Put only 1/8 of a tbsp. in a little bowl. Add 1 black pepper, oil, and salt. Stir all of it together. Now rub the mix all over the fish. Allow the fish to sit in the fridge for half an hour.
2. On some heavy duty aluminum foil coat it with cooking spray. Poke a few holes into the foil so the smoke can flow through. Place the fish on the foil, and arrange a couple of the lemon slices on it as well.
3. Smoke until the fish flakes have begun to form. Serve right afterward.

Smoke Time: 20 Mins

Smoke Temp: 225°

Ingredients:

2 dried habanero chilies

1 tbsp. peanut or vegetable oil

1 tbsp. salt

1/2 tbsp. freshly ground black pepper

1 (3-lb.) striped bass fillet (about 1 inch thick)

1 lemon, thinly sliced

Smoked Trout

Do you have a lot of trout from your last fishing trip? Well, here's a way to serve them up for dinner with a decadent style. Crumple some bay leaves on top to achieve a harmony of blending spices.

Ingredients:

2 cups water

1/3 cup plus 4 1/2 tsp. fine salt

1/2 cup packed light brown sugar

1 bay leaf, crumbled

1 tbsp. black peppercorns

1 1/2 lb.s boneless, skin-on whole trout (about 3 to 4), rinsed and butterflied

Vegetable oil

Serves: 2
Preparation Time: 15 minutes

Directions:

1. Put the peppercorns, water, bay leaf, salt, and brown sugar in a small saucepan. Bring it to medium heat, and cook the mixture until the sugar has been dissolved. Allow it to cool back down to room temperature for 20 minutes.
2. Store this brine mixture in a re-sealable plastic bag. Add the trout in the back, seal it up, and then store in the fridge for two hours.
3. Take the fish out of the brine, rinse it off, and be sure to pat it dry with some paper towels.
4. Put the fish in the smoker. The trout should start to turn an amber color, and once it begins to flake it means it's done. Serve while still warm.

Smoke Time: 30 Mins

Smoke Temp: 250°

BEEF

Smoked Steak Strips

Steak strips go great with some fried rice, or on top of some steamed vegetables. They're easy to smoke, and come out juicy when smoked. After these steak strips are smoked, they will have a rich, bronze coating which indicates they're ready to eat.

Ingredients:

2 tsp. freshly ground black pepper

1 tbsp. garlic powder

1/2 tbsp. salt

1/4 tbsp. dry mustard

2 (12-ounce) New York strip or sirloin strip steaks, trimmed

2 tsp. Worcestershire sauce

Serves: 6
Preparation Time: 15 minutes

Directions:

1. Combine the mustard, pepper, salt, and garlic powder all in one small bowl. Rub this on both sides of the steak strips. Place these coated pieces in a plastic bag. Toss in the Worcestershire sauce. Seal to coat the sauce all over the steak strips, and seal. Allow them to marinate in the fridge for half an hour.
2. Arrange the steaks on the rack of the smoker. In a spare pan pour two cups of water into it, and place it in the smoker over a place that doesn't have direct heat.
3. Close the lid of the smoker and allow steaks to smoke.
4. Once the steaks are done serve over rice or with some steamed vegetables.

Smoke Time: 1 Hour, 15 Mins

Smoke Temp: 225°

Slow Smoked Porterhouse Steaks

Who doesn't love a nice, thick, juicy steak? This is great if you're just getting into using your smoker, but need a basic recipe to build up from. Feel free to add in your favorite rub or marinade to this recipe. Or just eat it as is for a simple, but savory steak.

Serves: 4
Preparation Time: 15 minutes

Directions:

1. On each steak, season them on both sides with salt and pepper.
2. Place the steaks on a cutting board, and insert metal skewers, at least 3 or 4 so the steaks are secure. Afterwards turn the steaks to the side so the skewers are holding them upright.
3. Place steaks in the smoker. The internal temperatures of the steaks should be 120 degrees, and then they're ready to eat.

Smoke Time: 2 Hours

Smoke Temp: 200°

Ingredients:

2 whole porterhouse steaks, at least 1 1/2 inches thick (30 to 40 ounces each)

Kosher salt

freshly ground black pepper

Smoked Ultimate Flank Steak

This is the ultimate flank steak you won't find anywhere else. Once soaked in wine, and topped off with just a few choice spices, it comes out tender as can be. You barely have to cut into it since the meat splits so easily.

Ingredients:

1 1/2-2 lbs flank steaks

1/4 cup madeira wine

1/4 cup olive oil

1 tbsp. lemon pepper

1/2 tbsp. black pepper

1 tbsp. sea salt or 1 tbsp. kosher salt

1/8 cup soy sauce or 1/8 cup Worcestershire sauce

3 garlic cloves, crushed

1/2 tbsp. marjoram

Serves: 3
Preparation Time: 20 minutes

Directions:

1. Put the steak in a bag. Add in the rest of the ingredients, and shake around to coat the steak evenly.
2. Allow the steak to marinate for 6 to 12 hours. During the time it's marinating, be sure to turn the steak over at least four times.
3. Smoke the steak. Once done serve with preferred sides.

Smoke Time: 1 ½ Hours

Smoke Temp: 250°

Sweet Cola Ribs

These ribs have a sweeter taste than their spicier counterparts. Cola is used for the base of the barbecue sauce, and softens the meat so it's nice and tender. The meat will be falling off the bones once they're done smoking.

Serves: 4
Preparation Time: 15 minutes

Directions:

1. Head up a medium sauce pan over medium heat. Add in the oil. Once it's heated up, add onion and garlic. Sauté them until they become tender. Add the rest of the sauce ingredients, and bring it all to a boil. Reduce the heat, and then allow it to simmer for one hour and fifteen minutes.
2. In a small bowl, combine all the dry rub ingredients.
3. Rinse the ribs off. Be sure to dry them. Pull off any excess membrane or fat from the ribs. Season both sides as much as you please with the dry rub and sauce. Be sure to store the ribs in the fridge for four to twelve hours.
4. Place the ribs in the smoker. Flip them a couple of times while they're smoking.
5. Serve ribs while still warm.

Smoke Time: 1 Hour, 15 Mins

Smoke Temp: 250°

Ingredients:

Sweet Cola Barbecue Sauce:

1 tbsp. vegetable oil

1 medium onion, finely chopped

3 cloves garlic, finely chopped

2 cups ketchup

1 can cola

1/2 cup apple cider vinegar

2 tsp. brown sugar

1/2 tbsp. fresh ground black pepper

1/2 tbsp. onion powder

1/2 tbsp. ground mustard

1/2 tbsp. lemon juice

1 tbsp. Worcestershire sauce

Dry Rub:

2 tsp. salt

2 tsp. brown sugar

2 tsp. garlic powder

2 tsp. onion powder

1 tbsp. ground cumin

1 tbsp. chili powder

1 tbsp. black pepper

2 racks pork spare ribs (about 3 lb. each)

Easy Peasy Smoked Ribs

These ribs are excellent for any beginners with a smoker. All you need is a few basic ingredients to make you some of the best baby back ribs ever. They come out steaming, the meat is tender, and they taste like award winning baby back ribs.

Ingredients:

1 - 2 racks baby back pork ribs

1 - 8 oz bottle Kraft honey hickory smoke barbecue sauce

Sweet & Smokey Rub

Steak Seasoning

1/2 - cup brown sugar

Olive Oil

Serves: 2
Preparation Time: 15 minutes

Directions:

1. Cut the membrane off the ribs.
2. Rub the olive oil over the ribs on both sides. Apply the dry rub to the ribs and the steak seasoning.
3. Place the ribs in the fridge after wrapping them up in plastic wrap. Store them in the fridge for six hours or overnight.
4. Allow the rips to sit out for half an hour prior to smoking them.
5. Place a piece of foil on the rack. Place the ribs in the smoker, and allow them to smoke for two and a half hours.
6. Slather the ribs with barbecue sauce. Add some brown sugar to the barbecue sauce to make the ribs sweeter. Wrap them up in foil afterward.
7. Allow the ribs to cool for a few minutes before eating.

Smoke Time: 1 Hour

Smoke Temp: 225°

Memphis Style Beef Ribs

This is a different way to prepare ribs for a Memphis style taste. A smoky the fragrance from the other spices will rise up. Paprika sprinkled over the top will give the ribs a little kick to them. Once done, the perfect blend of spices all comes together in a perfect melody to your palette.

Serves: 4
Preparation Time: 15 minutes

Directions:

1. In a small bowl mix together all the dry rub ingredients. This rub can be used on multiple ribs or store for later.
2. Rinse the ribs off and dry them. Apply the dry rub to the ribs. Wrap them up in plastic wrap and store in the fridge for eight hours.
3. Place ribs in the smoker.
4. After the first two hours turn the ribs over. Allow them to smoke for the rest of the allotted time.
5. Serve while still warm.

Smoke Time: 2 Hours, 45 Mins

Smoke Temp: 250°

Ingredients:

BBQ Dry Rub:

1 1/2 cups paprika

3/4 cup sugar

3 3/4 tsp. onion powder

4 (about 4 lb.s each) slabs beef spare ribs

Smoked Burgers

During the summer burgers are on the menu at the family barbeque. While these smoked burgers keep it simple they still come out juicy and lip smacking delicious. Just top off each finished burger with a slice of provolone cheese, and let it melt for the best burgers this side of the equator.

Ingredients:

4 Hamburger Patties (hand shaped, using your preferred ground beef)

4 slices Provolone Cheese

Season All

Large Onion (with a beef bullion cube and a pat of butter)

Vlasic Farmers Garden Pickle Chips

Serves: 4
Preparation Time: 10 minutes

Directions:

1. Sprinkle the season all on each side of the burger patties.
2. Cut the onion into slices. In a foil square, place the onion in the middle. Do the same for a buillion cube and some butter. Seal up the foil.
3. Put the patties and onion inside the smoker.
4. Serve the burgers up with the cooked onion on top, pickle chips, mustard, and provolone cheese.

Smoke Time: 30 Mins

Smoke Temp: 250°

Triple Smoked Burger

Need the one burger to rule them all? This is a triple smoked monster of a burger dripping with a litany of flavors combined into the meat patties. While it's smoking the drip and sizzle of the juices hitting the coals will send up a fragrance that will make your mouth water.

Serves: 1
Preparation Time: 20 minutes

Directions:

1. Puree your mayo, 1 tbsp. of chipotle, and mustard in a blender. Place in a small bowl.
2. Cook the bacon in a small skillet over some medium heat. Transfer the bacon to some paper towels to drain once they're crispy.
3. Mix the beef with 1 tsp. of salt, 1 tbsp. chipotle, and paprika. Do the exact same for the other patties.
4. Brush some olive oil on the avocado and onion. Do this for both sides.
5. Place avocado slices on the rack of the smoker. Turn them only once, giving each of them 30 seconds to smoke.
6. Place the patties on the smoker. Halfway through flip them over.
7. Spread some sauce on the buns and top with cilantro, lettuce, avocado, bacon, onion, and the patties.

Smoke Time: 12 – 15 Mins

Smoke Temp: 250°

Ingredients:

1/2 cup mayonnaise

1 1/2 tsp. Dijon mustard

2 tsp. minced chipotle in adobo, including some sauce, divided

8 bacon slices

1 1/2 lb.s ground beef chuck (not lean)

2 tsp. sweet smoked paprika

1 large red onion, cut into 4 (1/2-inch) thick rounds, each stuck with a wooden pick to keep it together

1 firm-ripe avocado, quartered lengthwise, peeled, and cut lengthwise into 1/3-inch thick slices

Olive oil for brushing on onion and avocado

4 hamburger buns, grilled or toasted

Hickory Smoked Burgers

These burgers only use a little bit of tabasco sauce, but it makes all the difference. Juicy and savory, these hickory smoked burgers are huge crowd pleasers. Add in the onion soup mix and bread crumbs, and you have an unusual burger combination that tastes amazing when done.

Ingredients:

2 lb.s lean ground round (can use ground turkey for a low-fat burger)

1 package dry onion soup mix

1/2 cup water

1 tbsp. hot sauce

3/4 cup bread crumbs (if desired)

Worcestershire sauce

Serves: 12
Preparation Time: 15 minutes

Directions:

1. Place all the ingredients in a large bowl and mix together.
2. Roll the beef into patties it should yield 12 to 14 of them.
3. Place the patties in the smoker. Flip over halfway through smoking.
4. When they're ready serve immediately.

Smoke Time: 20 Mins

Smoke Temp: 250°

Smoked Beef Brisket

Beef brisket is a delicacy everyone should try at least ones. Fans of beef brisket will be delighted to try the smoked version of it. As the fragrance wafts out from the smoker as the brisket smokes mouths are sure to water. A simple blend of spices make this beef brisket a decadent dish to enjoy.

Serves: 6
Preparation Time: 10 minutes

Directions:

1. In a small bowl mix together all dry ingredients. Be sure they are blended very well.
2. Trim ¼ inch of fat from the brisket. Be sure to season the brisket with only ¼ cup of the rub you made earlier.
3. Smoke the brisket over indirect heat. Flip it over halfway into smoking.
4. Once the brisket is done, allow it to cool for ten minutes before serving.

Smoke Time: 7 Hours

Smoke Temp: 250°

Ingredients:

1 1/2 cups paprika

3/4 cup sugar

3 tsp. onion powder

3 tsp. garlic salt

1 tsp. celery salt

1 tsp. black pepper

1 tbsp. lemon pepper

1 tbsp. mustard powder

1 tbsp. cayenne

1/2 tbsp. dried thyme

1 trimmed brisket, about 5 to 6 lb.s

KICKING UP THE FLAVOR

Smoked Cherries

Cherries are sweet with just a hint of a sour tang to them. Once smoked these can either be eaten as a treat, or added on top of steak for extra flavoring. Whatever you choose it's bound to be an experience in fruit cuisine.

Serves: 1
Preparation Time: 5 minutes

Ingredients:

3 cups cherries or 3 cups fruit, of choice

12 ounces beer or 12 ounces apple juice

Directions:

1. Soak the wood chips you're going to use in the beer or apple juice.
2. Arrange the cherries in a single layer over the disposable pan.
3. Only add the fruit to any meat you're cooking two hours before you have to take it out. If not, allow the fruit to smoke for two hours before eating it.

Smoke Time: 2 Hours

Smoke Temp: 160°

Smoked Maple Butter Soaked Apples

These apples carry the flavor of fall within them, and are sure to warm up even the coldest of days. As the maple syrup slowly soaks into the apples a warm fragrance will rise up out of them. When these apples are done smoking they have a creamy tang to them people can't get enough of.

Ingredients:

Butter

Brown sugar

Maple syrup

4 apples

Serves: 4
Preparation Time: 10 minutes

Directions:

1. Be sure to core the apples before placing them on the grill. It's basically a hole in the top of the apple to add in the maple syrup, butter, and brown sugar.
2. Fill each apple up in the middle with the brown sugar, maple syrup, and butter.
3. Place a drip pan beneath the apples.
4. Arrange the apples on the rack together.
5. Once the apples are done smoking give them a few minutes to cool before eating.

Smoke Time: 1 ½ Hours

Smoke Temp: 350°

Smoked Eggs

No more waiting for hard boiled eggs to finish boiling in the pot! These smoked eggs shrink while they smoke, and turn a beautiful bronze color when they're done. The inside of the eggs is tender, firm, but with a slight creaminess sure to please.

Serves: 6
Preparation Time: 10 minutes

Directions:

1. Place your eggs on top of the grate.
2. Allow the eggs to smoke.
3. Give the eggs a few minutes to cool before eating them.

Smoke Time: 2 Hours

Smoke Temp: 230°

Ingredients:

Eggs (as many as you want)

Smoked Bananas

This is a simple, but awesome way to smoke some bananas. The cinnamon and honey, with the combination of a few teaspoons of lemon juice are sure to be a classic favorite. The cinnamon and lemon juice help to bring out the natural sweetness of the bananas. Once done the bananas melt in your mouth like warm ice cream.

Ingredients:

4 bananas unpeeled cut in half lengthwise

4 tsp liquid honey

4 tsp lemon juice 5 ml

1 tsp ground cinnamon

4 tbsp sliced almonds

Cooking oil

Serves: 4
Preparation Time: 15 minutes

Directions:

1. Put the bananas on the rack.
2. Afterwards, take the bananas out of the smoker. Remove their skins. Transfer them to a baking sheet that has oil spread on it.
3. Spread a ½ tsp. of lemon juice and honey each on one of each of your banana halves. Also add ½ alam. of almonds and 1/8 tsp. of cinnamon.
4. Start your oven up, and place your bananas in the broiler for about five minutes. Do this until they turn golden brown.

Smoke Time: 30 Mins

Smoke Temp: 200°

Smoked Oysters with Olive Relish

On those bad days, everyone needs a little comfort food to help turn a frown upside down. So brighten up a cloudy day with these succulent oysters. The basil and plum tomato give them an extra kick of flavor. The meat of these oysters is guaranteed to be firm, but creamy.

Serves: 1
Preparation Time: 15 minutes

Directions:

1. In a small bowl mix together the olives, black pepper, lemon juice, capers, olive oil, fresh basil, and the plum tomato.
2. On a aluminum foil pan, poke holes in the bottom with a knife or fork. Put another foil pan, but with no holes in it, on an unheated part of the smoker. Pour two cups of water in the pan with no holes in it.
3. Put your oysters in the pan with the holes in it.
4. Once they're done smoking drizzle 1 ½ tsp. of your olive mixture on your oysters. Serve the oysters with your lemon wedges.

Smoke Time: 9 Mins

Smoke Temp: 300°

Ingredients:

1/2 cup chopped pitted alamata olives

1/2 cup chopped seeded peeled plum tomato

2 tsp. chopped fresh basil

2 tsp. extra-virgin olive oil

1 tbsp. capers

1 tbsp. fresh lemon juice

1/2 tbsp. freshly ground black pepper

24 large shucked oysters (on the half shell)

12 lemon wedges

Smoked Paprika Roasted Potatoes

Roasted potatoes are a staple for any barbeque. They can be served as a side or eaten as a main dish. These roasted potatoes come out crispy on the outside, and soft on the inside.

Ingredients:

2 lbs. red potatoes

1 1/2 tbsp extra virgin olive oil

1 1/4 tsp smoked paprika

1 clove fresh garlic, minced very fine

3/4 tsp salt

1/4 tsp black pepper

Serves: 4
Preparation Time: 15 minutes

Directions:

1. Be sure to scrub your potatoes clean. Don't peel them. Slice each of the potatoes in wedges.
2. Once the potatoes are cut up, throw them all into a large zipper bag. Add in the olive oil. Be sure to toss the potatoes while they're in the bag.
3. Sprinkle your garlic and other spices into the bag. Shake it again so all the wedges are equally coated.
4. On a disposable foil pan spray it with some cook spray. Arrange your potato wedges on it in one single layer.
5. Allow the potatoes to smoke until they're crisp. Once they're done, allow them to cool for a few minutes before sprinkling some paprika over the top. Enjoy!

Smoke Time: 1Hour

Smoke Temp: 300°

Smoked Corn Recipe

This corn is smoldering with the butter and thyme. Smoked in its own husk this helps to hold in the butter, and allows it absorb into the corn. So when you take that first bite it's a sensation of the perfect corn on the cob made right.

Serves: 4
Preparation Time: 10 minutes

Directions:

1. In a small bowl combine the thyme and butter.
2. If not don't already, take the husks off of the corn. Throw away the silk on the corn.
3. Rub your butter mixture over the corn. Pull the husks back over your corn.
4. Place the corn in the smoker.
5. Allow the husks to sit for 10 minutes before serving them.

Smoke Time: 40 Mins

Smoke Temp: 250°

Ingredients:

1/2 cup butter, softened

2 tsp. chopped fresh thyme

8 ears fresh corn with husks

Smoked Asparagus

Asparagus is a popular food item which can be served alongside steak, chicken, pork ribs, and just about any other food under the sun. The snap of the stalk as you that first bite promises you another delicious mouthful. Asparagus goes great with some garlic mashed potatoes and steamed broccoli.

Ingredients:

2 tsp. butter

4 cloves garlic, sliced thin

2 tsp. lemon juice

salt to taste

1/4 tbsp. ground black pepper

1 onion, thinly sliced

1 1/2 lb.s asparagus, trimmed

Serves: 2
Preparation Time: 15 minutes

Directions:

1. In a small saucepan add in the garlic, and melt the butter.
2. Once the garlic is tender, take the saucepan from heat. Add in the black pepper, lemon juice, and salt.
3. Place the onions in a heat resistant container. Arrange the asparagus over the onions. Drizzle your garlic and butter mix over the asparagus.
4. Place in the smoker. Once done serve while still warm.

Smoke Time: 1 Hour

Smoke Temp: 240°

Smoked Bacon

For this recipe, all you need is bacon. You can either serve it alongside some eggs for a camp style breakfast, or use it to top off some amazing burgers. The pop and crackle as this bacon smokes promises only the finest in bacon cuisine. When it's done it comes out crisp and flavorful.

Serves: 4
Preparation Time: 10 minutes

Ingredients:

10 slices of thick bacon

Directions:

1. Bring your smoker up to 225 degrees.
2. Arrange the bacon on a single layer of aluminum foil. Poke some holes in the aluminum so the smoke can flow through.
3. Place the bacon in the smoker.
4. Let the bacon to cool for a few minutes before serving.

Smoke Time: 30 Mins

Smoke Temp: 225°

Smoked Salmon Cucumbers

If you need simple, healthy appetizers this is the way to go. Once you pop them into your mouth it's easy to see why salmon and cucumbers make the perfect balance of flavors. The cucumbers are crisp, and the salmon brings it into harmony with the cream cheese. A finger food that is made to make taste buds everywhere rejoice.

Ingredients:

1 large English cucumber

1 carton (8 ounces) spreadable chive and onion cream cheese

7 to 8 ounces smoked salmon or lox, chopped

Minced chives

Serves: 6
Preparation Time: 10 minutes

Directions:

1. Smoke the salmon for the allotted time.
2. Chop the salmon up. Peel your cucumber and cut it into slices that are ¼ inch.
3. Spread some cream cheese on the slices of cucumber.
4. Place a piece of salmon on top of each cucumber slice. Be sure to sprinkle with chives. Serve immediately or store in the fridge for later.

Smoke Time: 25 Mins

Smoke Temp: 225°

Roasted Broccoli

Who says broccoli can't be smoked? With just a few extra seasonings this broccoli tastes absolutely amazing. As the steam rolls off these babies you'll be hard pressed not to sneak a bite before serving them up.

Serves: 2
Preparation Time: 15 minutes

Directions:

1. In a large bowl put your broccoli in it. Add the pepper, lemon juice, salt, and oil together. Drizzle this mixture over your broccoli. Toss everything if necessary to coat it all. Allow the broccoli to stand for half an hour.
2. Be sure to toss your broccoli one last time before draining out the marinade. Place the cheese in a big Ziploc bag. Place the broccoli inside as well. Shake everything together so the broccoli is evenly coated.
3. Coat the grill rack on the inside of the smoker with oil. Arrange the broccoli on the drill directly over a drip pan.
4. Allow the broccoli to smoke and turn it over halfway through smoking.
5. Serve while still warm. Feel free to garnish with some fresh basil or shaved parmesan.

Smoke Time: 10 Mins

Smoke Temp: 250°

Ingredients:

6 cups fresh broccoli spears

2 tsp. plus 1-1/2 tsp. lemon juice

2 tsp. olive oil

1/4 tbsp. salt

1/4 tbsp. pepper

3/4 cup grated Parmesan cheese

Shaved Parmesan cheese

purple basil leaves (Optional)

Smoke Roasted Sweet Potatoes

When these sweet potatoes start smoking it's hard to resist the urge to sneak a taste. The salt defines the sweetness in the potatoes. A sprinkle of pepper also gives it a spicy way to enhance the flavor.

Ingredients:

4 large sweet potatoes (6 to 8 oz. each)

4 tsp. (½ stick) salted butter, melted

Coarse salt (kosher or sea) and freshly ground black pepper

2 tsp. maple syrup

2 tsp. brown sugar, for serving

Serves: 4
Preparation Time: 15 minutes

Directions:

1. Be sure to clean the sweet potatoes off very well. Pat them dry with paper towels. Put the potatoes in a drip pan. Pour only 2 tbsp. of butter onto your potatoes. Be sure all the sides are coated. Season your potatoes liberally with the salt and pepper.
2. Put the drip pan underneath the grate.
3. Brush the grill of the smoker with some oil before arranging the potatoes on it. Close the smoker and allow the potatoes to smoke. The flesh of your potatoes should be browned, and the flesh tender.
4. Once the sweet potatoes are done, be sure to cut them in half, but lengthwise. Spread the last of the butter and some maple syrup over the potatoes. At this point also sprinkle some brown sugar over the top of the potatoes. Season liberally with salt and pepper for taste.
5. The sweet potatoes can be eaten at this point, even with the skin on.

Smoke Time: 1 Hour

Smoke Temp: 400°

Smoked Brussel Sprouts

Brussel sprouts taste a little strong, but this will help to soften the taste. The mustard and paprika give them a zing. Combine that with the olive oil to soften them up, and you can sink a fork into them to enjoy on a summer afternoon.

Serves: 4
Preparation Time: 10 minutes

Directions:

1. Be sure to cut the stems off of the Brussel sprouts.
2. Put all the Brussel sprouts in a large bowl and place them in the microwave. Microwave them on high for three minutes.
3. Add salt, olive oil, paprika, garlic, and mustard to the bowl. Mix it all together so they combine well. Let the sprouts cool down for a few minutes before handling them again.
4. Stick 4 to 5 brussel sprouts each on a metal skewer.
5. Place the Brussel sprouts in the smoker. Turn them over halfway through smoking.
6. Put the Brussel sprouts back in the bowl again and toss them with the last of the garlic and oil mixture.

Smoke Time: 10 Mins

Smoke Temp: 225°

Ingredients:

1 lb. Brussels sprouts, as uniform in size as possible*

2 tsp. olive oil

1 tbsp. minced garlic

1 tbsp. dry mustard

1 tbsp. smoked paprika

1 tbsp. kosher salt

1/4 tbsp. freshly ground black pepper

Smoked Artichokes

Artichokes are packed with plenty of nutrients your body needs. When you smoke them you can either eat them as they are, or mash them up to make your own version of guacamole. These smoked artichokes come out soft, tender, and warm. A squeeze of lemon and spices brings it altogether into a melody of flavors.

Ingredients:

2 to 4 large globe artichokes

1 lemon, cut into wedges

1/3 cup olive oil

1 tbsp. of chopped fresh herbs such as rosemary, oregano, and thyme

Salt

Serves: 2
Preparation Time: 10 minutes

Directions:

1. In a small bowl place the olive oil and chopped herbs. Place the bowl in the microwave, and heat it up for 30 seconds.
2. In a large pot, heat up an inch of water. Place the steamer rack in there. If you cut off any part of the artichokes, be sure to rub the cut with a lemon wedge. This will prevent the artichoke from turning brown.
3. Peel away the thick outer layer of the artichoke stem. Trim the stems down so they're only two inches away from the base.
4. Cut off ½ inch of the artichoke at the top. Be sure to cut the entire artichoke in half, and repeat this for each vegetable. Use a spoon to scoop out any inner choke leaves and the fuzzy chokes. Rub your lemon juice over any and every exposed cut area as well on the vegetables.
5. When the water comes to a boil in the pot, put all the artichokes on the steam rack. Be sure the cut sides are down. Cover the pot up, and allow the artichokes to steam for 20 minutes.
6. Put the artichokes on the smoker, and brush each artichoke with your herb oil you made. Sprinkle some salt onto the artichokes as well.
7. When you go to serve the artichokes, sprinkle the cut sides with another bit of lemon juice. Eat with some mayo or aioli.

Smoke Time: 10 Mins

Smoke Temp: 300°

SIDES

Smoked Vegetables

Even vegetables can taste amazing when prepared on the smoker. You can either smoke all these together in a pan, or stick them on a kebab to sizzle in the smoker. They will be tender, crispy, and above all an excellent edition alongside some ribs or a steak.

Ingredients:

1 ear of fresh corn, husks and silks removed

1 medium yellow squash, cut into ½ inch thick slices

1 small red onion, cut into thin wedges

1 small green pepper, cunt into 1 inch strips

1 small red pepper, cut into 1 inch strips

1 cup mushrooms, halved

2 tbsp. vegetable oil

2 tbsp. chicken seasoning

Serves: 6
Preparation Time: 15 minutes

Directions:

1. In a large bowl toss the vegetables with some oil. Sprinkle the chicken seasoning over them. Place all the vegetables in a grill basket.
2. Place vegetables in the smoker. Be sure to turn them every few minutes.
3. Once done the vegetables will be tender. Serve while still warm.

Smoke Time: 12 Mins

Smoke Temp: 250°

Four Cheese Smoked Mac 'n' Cheese

This creamy mac 'n' cheese is melt in your mouth delicious. It's savory, and combines four cheeses to give you that childhood favorite everyone grew up with. Sprinkle some bacon bits on the top for extra bit of flavor to make this a real treat.

Serves: 4
Preparation Time: 15 minutes

Directions:

1. Be sure to cook the past first according to the directions. Get a medium sauce pan, melt the butter, and then be sure to whisk the flour with the butter. Allow it to cook over a medium heat for only two minutes. Whisk a in the milk. Bring it all to a boil for five minutes. Add in the cream cheese, stirring until the entire mixture has become smooth. Next, add in the pepper and salt.
2. Get a large bowl. Mix together cream sauce, 1 cup cheddar, 1 cup gouda cheese, pasta, and parmesan cheese. Transfer the mixture to an aluminum roasting pan. Sprinkle all the leftover gouda and cheddar cheese on top of the mixture.
3. Place the mac 'n' cheese in the smoker.
4. It should turn brown and be bubbly once done. Serve while still warm.

Smoke Time: 1 Hour

Smoke Temp: 225°

Ingredients:

(16-ounce) package elbow macaroni

1/4 cup butter

1/4 cup all-purpose flour

3 cups milk

1 (8-ounce) package cream cheese, cut into large chunks

1 tbsp. salt

1/2 tbsp. black pepper

2 cups (8 ounces) extra sharp Cheddar cheese, shredded

2 cups (8 ounces) Gouda cheese, shredded

1 cup (4 ounces) Parmesan cheese, shredded

Bacon-Wrapped Cheesy Stuffed Jalapenos

Stuffed jalapenos are spicy! They may make your eyes water, and cause your mouth to burn a little. However, these babies are packed to the brim with cheese and crispy bacon. They have a nice little crunch when you bite into them, and people are quickly going to asking for these again!

Ingredients:

12 fresh jalapeño peppers

8 ounces cream cheese, softened to room temperature

1 cup shredded cheddar cheese

1 clove garlic, chopped

1/2 tbsp. smoked paprika

12 slices bacon, cut in half

Serves: 4
Preparation Time: 15 minutes

Directions:

1. Cut each of the jalapeno peppers lengthwise. Take out the center membrane and seeds.
2. Combine the paprika, cream cheese, garlic, and cheddar cheese together. Add salt for taste. Spoon this mixture into the cut peppers.
3. Wrap each of the jalapeno peppers in a half slice of bacon. Stick a toothpick through each one to keep them in place.
4. Place the jalapenos in the smoker
5. Serve immediately after they're done smoking.

Smoke Time: 45 Mins

Smoke Temp: 300°

Wicked Baked Beans

These baked beans do indeed have a wicked taste. Easy to make, and excellent for those cold days in fall when you need something creamy and warm to fill you up. If you're looking for an extra kick in flavor smoke the bacon first before adding it to the beans.

Serves: 24
Preparation Time: 15 minutes

Directions:

1. In a skillet be sure to cook the bacon until it's crisp or smoke it.
2. Sauté the onion, bell pepper, and jalapeno until tender.
3. Be sure to combine all ingredients.
4. In a baking pan pour all the ingredients into it.
5. Place the beans in the smoker.
6. When the beans are ready either serve right away, or cover up and save for later.

Smoke Time: 2 ½ Hours

Smoke Temp: 250°

Ingredients:

1/2 lb bacon (cut into 1/2-inch squares)

1/2 medium onion, diced

1/2green bell pepper, diced

1 -2 jalapeno, diced (seeding is optional depending on desired heat)

1 (55 ounce) canbush's original baked beans or 1 (55 ounce) canbush's maple baked beans

8 ounces canned crushed pineapple, drained

1 cup dark brown sugar, firmly packed

1 cup ketchup

1/2 tbsp. ground dry mustard

Smoked Trout Potato Skins

Trout has a soft texture to it that combines well with the crunch of the potato skins. These are similar to double baked potatoes, but with a few variations to make them unique. So please enjoy this little delicacy of a side with friends and family.

Ingredients:

8 (3-inch-long) russet potatoes (about 2 1/4 lb.s), scrubbed and thoroughly dried

2 tsp. unsalted butter (1/4 stick), melted

Kosher salt

Freshly ground black pepper

1 tbsp. grapeseed or vegetable oil

1/2 tbsp. lime juice

2 cups baby arugula, washed and dried

1 cup Smoked Trout Pâté

Serves: 4
Preparation Time: 15 minutes

Directions:

1. Be sure to pierce each potato with a fork. Place on the rack in the smoker, and allow them to smoke for two hours. Once they're done, place they on a wire rack. Allow them to cool for ten minutes so you can handle them.
2. Cut each potato lengthwise. Scoop out all the flesh of the potato, leaving only ¼ inch of the meat inside intact. Coat the insides of the potato with melted butter, pepper, and salt. Do the same for the skin of the potato on both sides.
3. Place potatoes back in the smoker, and allow them to smoke for about six to ten minutes.
4. In a medium bowl mix together lime juice and oil. Add in the arugula at this point. Mix it with the mixture. Divide this mixture among the skins. Top each one off with a tbsp. of the trout pate. Place back in the smoker, and smoke for an additional 5 minutes. Serve afterwards.

Smoke Time: 2 Hours, 5 Mins

Smoke Temp: 300°

Smoked Potato Salad

Potato salad is a classic for a Sunday dinner or a barbeque. If you're looking to add a little bit of flavor to a lazy afternoon this potato salad is sure to have you picking up the spoon for seconds. Soft, creamy, and just a little bit of an extra tang to keep it all interesting.

Serves: 4
Preparation Time: 15 minutes

Directions:

1. Mix together potatoes, 1 tbsp. oil, salt, and pepper in a medium bowl. Toss everything to coat them.
2. Arrange all the potatoes on a foil pan in one layer. Close the lid of the smoker once you put the potatoes in there.
3. Once done, take the potatoes out and transfer them to a medium bowl. Mix together the onions and olives in the bowl with the potatoes.
4. Add in the parsley, oil, and the last of the ingredients into a small bowl. Stir it altogether with a whisk. Sprinkle this mixture over the potatoes. Toss to get them coated evenly, and serve.

Smoke Time: 30 Mins

Smoke Temp: 400°

Ingredients:

1/4 cup olive oil, divided

1/2 tbsp. black pepper

1/4 tbsp. kosher salt

1 1/2 lb.s small potatoes

1/3 cup sliced pitted kalamata olives

2 thinly sliced green onions

2 tsp. chopped fresh flat-leaf parsley

1 tbsp. red wine vinegar

2 tsp. celery seed

1 tbsp. Dijon mustard

Smoked Salmon Deviled Eggs

Deviled eggs are excellent as a quick finger food. Add in salmon, and it's hard to stop eating these creamy, smoky flavored appetizers. Just pop one in your mouth, and you'll see why everyone will is asking for more.

Ingredients:

8 extra-large eggs

1/2 cup sour cream

2 ounces cream cheese, at room temperature

2 tsp. good mayonnaise

1 tbsp. freshly squeezed lemon juice

2 tsp. minced fresh chives, plus extra for garnish

4 ounces good smoked salmon, minced

1 tbsp. kosher salt

1/2 tbsp. freshly ground black pepper

2 ounces salmon roe

Serves: 4
Preparation Time: 20 minutes

Directions:

1. In a large pot, bring water to a boil. Place the eggs in the pot, cover it up, and allow them to boil for 15 minutes. Drain the water from the pot and fill it again with cold water. Allow the eggs to cool.
2. Peel the shell off the eggs. Cut them in half, lengthwise only. Scoop the yolks out carefully with a spoon. Put the bowl of a electric mixer. Place the eggs whites on a platter and set them aside. Sprinkle them with a little bit of salt as well.
3. Add pepper, sour cream, salt, cream cheese, salmon, mayonnaise, chives, and lemon juice to the egg yolks. Beat them at a medium speed in the mixer so everything becomes fluffy. Use a small spoon to fill the eggs whites back up with the mixed egg yolk.
4. Cover the eggs loosely with plastic wrap, and then store them in the fridge for half an hour.
5. Add a dollop of salmon roe on top of the eggs.
6. Place the eggs on the smoker rack. Afterwards, sprinkle them with some pepper and salt before serving.

Smoke Time: 4 Mins

Smoke Temp: 225°

Smoked Cabbage

Cabbage is a staple in many salads, on burgers, and usually is not given a lot of attention. Here, you get it to where it's nice and crispy. There's a pleasant crunch when you take the first bite. The addition of a little bit of butter, and 3 bouillon cubes makes all the difference.

Serves: 2
Preparation Time: 10 minutes

Ingredients:

1 Whole cabbage

butter

2-3 chicken or beef bouillon cubes

Directions:

1. In the cavity of the cabbage, cut out a hole that is two to three inches big.

2. In the cavity, pack it with butter and bouillon cubes.

3. Use heavy duty foil to wrap up the cabbage, but not the top.

4. Place cabbage in smoker. Add more butter when needed.

5. Eat the cabbage once it's done.

Smoke Time: 5 Hours

Smoke Temp: 225°

Smoky Okra

Okra is a very popular food. People like them fried, dried, and may even eat them steamed. Smoked okra tastes even better, and is easy to prepare. A sprinkle of paprika and salt add just enough a spice to bring all the flavors into harmony with each other.

Ingredients:

1 lb. Okra

Smoked Paprika

1 tbsp. vegetable oil

¾ tsp. salt

Serves: 4
Preparation Time: 5 minutes

Directions:

1. Place the okra in a large bowl, and toss it with the oil, salt, and paprika.
2. Put the okra on 0wooden skewers.
3. Place the okra on the smoker. Turn the okra over halfway through smoking.
4. Once done eat it while it's still warm.

Smoke Time: 10 Mins

Smoke Temp: 225°

Naan

Naan is popular bread they eat in India. It's very soft, moist, and when smoked even a bit crispy. Combine this with some hummus as a dip and it doubles as a snack food too.

Serves: 6
Preparation Time: 10 minutes

Directions:

1. Get a large bowl, and dissolve the yeast in some warm water. Leave it to stand for ten minutes. Add in the flour, sugar, salt, egg, and milk. This will make the dough. Knead it for eight minutes on a surface that has been lightly floured.
2. Now place the dough in a boil that was rubbed with oil. Cover the top with a damp cloth, and place it aside. Allow the dough to rise for one hour.
3. Punch down on your dough. Knead in the garlic. Begin to pinch off handfuls of the dough. Roll them to the size of golf balls, and put on a tray. Cover them up with a towel, and allow them to rise for half an hour.
4. Once the dough is done rising place the dough in the smoker. It should be browned lightly. Brush the uncooked side with some butter. Turn the dough over halfway through.
5. Repeat step 4 until all the Naan is smoked.

Smoke Time: 6 Mins

Smoke Temp: 250°

Ingredients:

1 (.25 ounce) package active dry yeast

1 cup warm water

1/4 cup white sugar

3 tsp. milk

1 egg, beaten

2 tsp. salt

4 1/2 cups bread flour

2 tsp. minced garlic (optional)

1/4 cup butter, melted

Smoked Zucchini

During those warm summer months one of the best pleasures is the wave of fresh fruits and vegetables that come with it. If you have some extra zucchini available try making this healthy little snack. The zucchini will come out soft and crisp, making it a perfect on a sunny summer's day.

Ingredients:

1 large zucchini

1/4 cup Italian-style salad dressing

Serves: 1
Preparation Time: 5 minutes

Directions:

1. Cut the zucchini up into ¼ inch slices. In a large bowl toss it with the Italian dressing.
2. Bring the smoker up to 250 degrees.
3. Place the zucchini in the smoker.
4. Serve and eat.

Smoke Time: 5 Mins

Smoke Temp: 250°

Smoked Yellow Squash

Yellow squash is an excellent side with some steak and mashed potatoes. When the garlic becomes fragrant and is applied to the squash it enhances the flavor. While considered a very tender food, and melts on the tongue when you bite into it.

Serves: 4
Preparation Time: 15 minutes

Directions:

1. Cut your squash horizontally. Cut it into ¼ inch and ½ inch slices.
2. In a small pan heat up some garlic clove and olive oil over medium heat. Do this until the garlic starts to sizzle. Brush each slice of squash with this garlic oil. Add salt and pepper to taste.
3. Place the squash in the smoker on a rack. Flip it on its other side halfway through. Continue to brush with the garlic oil as needed.
4. Serve while still warm.

Smoke Time: 20 Mins

Smoke Temp: 250°

Ingredients:

4 medium yellow squash

1/2 cup extra virgin olive oil

2 cloves garlic, crushed

salt and pepper to taste

DESSERTS

Spice Cake

This cake takes the spice and makes it nice. It has a little bit of a spicy kick to it. Eaten with a cup of your favorite cappuccino it's excellent for those lazy afternoons when you want indulge your sweet tooth. When the cake is smoked it comes out light, fluffy, and delicious!

Serves: 4
Preparation Time: 20 minutes

Directions:

1. Get a small saucepan and melt the butter. Add in the brown sugar and honey, heat it through until the sugar has dissolved.
2. Get a large mixing bowl and mix together the nutmeg, flour, baking soda, and cinnamon. Add in the egg and butter mixture. Mix it all completely. Also add in the cherry brandy, almonds, and candied fruits.
3. On a baking sheet spread the batter over it
4. For the icing, in a small bowl mix together all the icing ingredients. Beat it until it's smooth.
5. Once the cake is done, remove it from the smoker. Allow it to cool before applying the icing.

Smoke Time: 20 Mins

Smoke Temp: 250°

Ingredients:

For the Cake:

2 tbsp. butter

2/3 cup honey

½ cup packed brown sugar

2 cups all-purpose flour

¾ tsp. ground cinnamon

½ tsp. baking soda

½ tsp nutmeg

1 egg

½ cup chopped almonds

½ cup chopped mixed candied fruits

2 tbsp. cherry brandy

For the lemon icing:

1 ½ cups powdered sugar

1 egg white

½ tsp. finely grated lemon zest

1 tsp. lemon juice

Berry Biscotti Crisp

This recipe uses a lot of berries! Whether you decide to use the sun loving strawberries, and the sweet loving blueberries, or even just a couple of tangy raspberries is completely up to you. Frozen berries or fresh berries can be used too!

Ingredients:

3 cups fresh or frozen blueberries

2 cups fresh or frozen strawberries

2/3 cup packed brown sugar, divided

½ all-purpose flour

½ tsp. ground cinnamon

Pinch of salt

¼ cup unsalted butter

½ cup almond biscotti

½ chopped toasted almonds

Serves: 4
Preparation Time: 15 minutes

Directions:

1. Get a large bowl, and mix together 1/3 cup of brown sugar and the berries. Divide this mixture among 8 aluminum cupcake cups.
2. In another bowl mix together the salt, flour, cinnamon, and the last of the brown sugar. Be sure to cut up the flour mixture so it starts to make small crumbles. Add in the almonds and cookies. Sprinkle this over the fruit in the cupcake cups.
3. Place all the cupcake cups into the smoker
4. They should come out lightly browned and bubbly.

Smoke Time: 25 Mins

Smoke Temp: 300°

Bananas Calypso

When the summer sun is high in the sky it's natural to want a cold treat to help cool you down. The dark rum, sugar, and lime help to make the banana calypso an exotic dessert. Soft, warm bananas combined with the cold ice cream are a nice way to beat the heat.

Serves: 4
Preparation Time: 15 minutes

Directions:

1. Combine the cinnamon, sugar, lime juice, and melted butter in a small bowl. Brush each of the banana's with only ¼ cup of this butter mixture.
2. Place the bananas in the smoker. Turn the bananas over halfway through the smoking process.
3. Once the bananas are done smoking, put them on a dish that is flameproof. Slice the bananas up, and pour the last of the butter mixture into the dish. Put the dish back in the smoker.
4. Allow the bananas to smoke for the rest of the time. After you remove the bananas from the smoker pour the rum over them.
5. Immediately serve the bananas with ice cream.

Ingredients:

1/3 cup sugar

¼ cup unsalted butter, melted

2 tbsp. lime juice

1 tsp. ground cinnamon

4 firm bananas, peeled

1/3 dark rum

4 scoops ice cream

Smoke Time: 10 Mins

Smoke Temp: 250°

Smoked Brownies

When you're on the smoker cooking away, why not pop some brownies in there? This version is a quick, easy way to have dessert on the table. These brownies come out crispy in a wave of chocolate goodness.

Ingredients:

1 cup brown sugar

1 cup butter

1 cup flour

1 egg

1 cup pecans

1 tbsp. vanilla

1 tsp. salt

1 cup chocolate chips

Serves: 4
Preparation Time: 15 minutes

Directions:

1. In a skillet, melt the butter. Transfer the other ingredients into a large mixing bowl and combine them. Add the melted butter. Mix this together.
2. Transfer this mixture to an aluminum pan. Place in the smoker.
3. Allow the brownies to smoke.
4. Serve them with a scoop of vanilla ice cream.

Smoke Time: 25 Mins

Smoke Temp: 350°

Nutella Smores

A campfire isn't always needed to enjoy some delicious s'mores! Crunchy graham crackers go perfect with the creamy chocolate as it begins to melt. Your marshmallows will turn a golden color once they're done.

Serves: 4
Preparation Time: 5 minutes

Directions:

1. Break each of the graham crackers in half.
2. Spread 1 tsp. of the Nutella on each cracker half.
3. Place a marshmallow on each cracker half.
4. Place in the smoker.
5. Enjoy while still hot.

Smoke Time: 5 Mins

Smoke Temp: 250°

Ingredients:

2 graham cracker slabs

4 tsp. nutella

4 large marshmallows

Smoked Peaches Drowning in Rum with Ice Cream

Peaches are naturally quite sweet. The rum gives these peaches a bit of an edge, but still retaining the soft texture of the peaches. Once warmed up and served with ice cream the rum's heady flavor combined with the peaches makes it a winner.

Ingredients:

2 peaches

1/3 cup Dark Rum

1 tbsp. lemon or lime juice

1 tbsp. vanilla

2 tsp. maple syrup

1/4 cup sugar

4 scoops vanilla ice cream

Serves: 4
Preparation Time: 15 minutes

Directions:

1. In a sauce pan pour in sugar, booze, molasses, lemon juice, and vanilla. Melt all of this over high heat. Stir the mixture, and boil it for 10 minutes. Allow it to cool afterward.
2. Cut each of the peaches in half, and remove the pits. Place them in the smoker. The skin should slide off.
3. In a bowl add a scoop of ice cream. Pour the mixture from the pan over it. Top it off with the peaches. Serve this immediately.

Smoke Time: 20 Mins

Smoke Temp: 250°

Pecan Tassies

Pecan tassies are very small, and even have a little bit of a crunch in them due to the almonds. They have a crisp, but soft texture to them. Once off the smoker they're warm and creamy.

Serves: 4
Preparation Time: 15 minutes

Directions:

1. Mix together the flour, cream cheese, and butter in a bowl.
2. Make balls that are 1 inch tall and place in a mini muffin pan. Be sure to press the balls down into the pan.
3. Whisk the melted butter, eggs, vanilla, and brown sugar. Pour this into the cups so it's 2/3 full.
4. Place in the smoker. Allow to cool for a few minutes before serving.

Smoke Time: 30 Mins

Smoke Temp: 350°

Ingredients:

Ingredients for the shells

3 ounces (1 small brick) full fat cream cheese

1 stick salted butter (8 tsp.) at room temp

1 cup all-purpose flour

Ingredients for the filling

1/3 cup pecans, coarsely chopped

1 egg

3/4 cup dark brown sugar

1/2 tbsp. vanilla

1 tbsp. salted melted butter

Smoked Avocados with Strawberry-Mango Salsa

The avocados will remain slightly firm doing the smoking process. The strawberry-mango salsa gives them additional flavoring. Once smoked these avocados come out smooth and creamy. A fork will literally sink right into them.

Ingredients:

4 not-fully-ripe avocados, just turning soft

1/4 cup honey

1/4 cup olive oil

1 medium mango, peeled, pitted, and cut into 1/2" cubes

1/2 lb. strawberries, cut into 1/2" cubes

1 tbsp. balsamic vinegar

1/3 cup orange juice

2 tsp. lemon juice

Lettuce leaves, for serving

Serves: 4
Preparation Time: 15 minutes

Directions:

1. Slice each of the avocados lengthwise. Remove the seeds. Get a small bowl, and with a whisk mix together the olive oil and honey. Brush this on the exposed parts of the avocados. Cover it up with plastic wrap and set aside.
2. Get a medium bowl and mix together lemon juice, mango, orange juice, strawberries, and vinegar.
3. Place the avocados in the smoker. Brush with the oil mixture and flip them over.
4. Place each avocado on a bed of lettuce. Fill each of the seed cavities with the fruit salsa you made earlier. Serve as is.

Smoke Time: 6 Mins

Smoke Temp: 325°

Smoked Cantaloupe

Cantaloupe is delicious on its own. Add some cracked pepper on top, drizzle some honey over it, and you have an exotic summer dessert. Only one spice is needed to make the tender meat of this fruit the decadent dish it truly is.

Serves: 4
Preparation Time: 5 minutes

Ingredients:

1 large cantaloupe

1/4 cup honey

1/4 cup lemon juice

2 tsp. cracked black pepper

Directions:

1. Stir together lemon and honey in a shallow dish.

2. Cut the cantaloupe into ½ inch slices that are round. Remove any pulp and seeds there are.

3. Place the slices in the smoker, and brush with the lemon and honey mixture.

4. Place on a platter. Brush with the honey mixture again, and sprinkle with a bit of cracked pepper.

Smoke Time: 3 Mins

Smoke Temp: 325°

Figs with Mascarpone and Smoked Chocolate Ganache

Figs are excellent alongside everyone's favorite treat chocolate. They're quick, easy to make and best of all have that little extra class to them. Enjoy the crunch of the fig and the warm texture of the chocolate.

Ingredients:

12 figs, cut in half lengthwise

1/3 cup mascarpone

Chocolate ganache

Serves: 4
Preparation Time: 10 minutes

Directions:

1. Cut the figs in half and wash them thoroughly. Thread the figs onto some wooden skewers.
2. Put the cut sides down in the smoker.
3. Once the figs have cooled for a few minutes, take them off the skewers.
4. Arrange over some chocolate ganache and top it all off with mascarpone.

Smoke Time: 2 Mins

Smoke Temp: 250°

Smoked Pineapple Sundae

On a warm day, it's natural to crave something cold to eat. A smoked pineapple piece is perfect for a bowl of cool, creamy ice cream. Once the pineapple is done smoking it will come out warm and juicy.

Serves: 1
Preparation Time: 10 minutes

Directions:

1. Mix together the cinnamon, brown sugar, lemon juice, and butter. Brush it over the pineapple slices.
2. Place the pineapple in the smoker.
3. Serve it with a scoop of ice cream.

Smoke Time: 2 Mins

Smoke Temp: 250°

Ingredients:

1 pineapple, peeled, cored and cut into 1 inch slices

1/2 cup brown sugar

2 tsp. melted butter

2 tsp. lemon juice

1 tbsp. cinnamon

1/2 gallon vanilla ice cream

CHEESES

Smoked Cheddar Cheese

This cheese will taste more robust once it's been smoked. Smoking the cheese can take a long time, but the results are satisfying. The smoke will seep into the cheese creating a delicacy you'll be eager to use in future recipes.

Serves: 2
Preparation Time: 5 minutes

Directions:

1. Keep the smoker at a low temperature so the cheese doesn't melt.
2. Place the cheese in the smoker.
3. Place it in a bag, and store in the fridge for two weeks.

Smoke Time: 4 Hours

Smoke Temp: 90°

Ingredients:

Two 8-ounce blocks Cheddar cheese

Smoked String Cheese

String cheese is fun to eat. Kids love the challenge of pulling the "strings" off to get a perfect string right down the middle. A smoky flavor can make them taste even better and even stored away for later for future lunches. Spices can be added to make your average string cheese even more flavorful.

Ingredients:

String cheese (as much as you want)

Serves: 4
Preparation Time: 5 minutes.

Directions:

1. The string cheese must be cold before being placed in the smoker.
2. Transfer to a plastic bag, and allow it to sit in the fridge for a day.

Smoke Time: 2 ½ Hours

Smoke Temp: 90°

Smoked Gouda Cheese

Once smoked, gouda cheese has a flavor reminiscent of bacon. It can be used in a number of different recipes. It will continue be firm and retain its natural flavor, but will enhance the texture from the smoke.

Serves: 4
Preparation Time: 5 minutes

Directions:

1. Place Gouda in the smoker.
2. Afterwards place smoked gouda cheese in a plastic bag. Store in the fridge for two weeks.

Smoke Time: 6 Hours

Smoke Temp: 90°

Ingredients:

1 lb. Gouda cheese (as much or less as you want)

Smoked Mozzarella

This cheese is excellent to use in future recipes. It has a little bit of a tang to it due to the salt and pepper, but it's also creamy. While it's melting the fragrance will have you planning to make more cheese in the near future.

Ingredients:

1 large ball mozzarella (about 1 lb.)

Vegetable oil, for brushing the cheesecloth

Salt

Freshly ground black pepper

Serves: 6
Preparation Time: 10 minutes

Directions:

1. In an aluminum pan, poke holes in the bottom. Put the cheesecloth on a flat surface. Brush the cloth with the vegetable oil. Season the cloth with the black pepper and salt. After this, put the mozzarella in the center of the cheese cloth and wrap it up.
2. Place the cheese in the aluminum pan.
3. Place the cheese in the smoker.
4. Once the cheese is done remove it from the smoker. Allow it to cool to room temperature.

Smoke Time: 40 Mins

Smoke Temp: 250°

Smoked Cheese Crisps

This is an excellent way to enjoy your favorite cheeses in a snack form. They're light, crispy, and crunchy. The golden brown at the edges promises a delightful combination of smoky flavor, and a hearty crunch similar to a potato chip.

Serves: 1
Preparation Time: 5 minutes

Ingredients:

1 block of cheese (can be literally any cheese)

Directions:

1. Cut the cheese into small cubes. Arrange on a baking sheet placed on an aluminum pan.
2. Arrange the cheeses on the pan.
3. Place cheeses in the smoker.
4. Place the pan on another one that has ice on it.
5. Mix in any spices you desire. Smoke for an additional five minutes, or until the edges turn brown. Allow the cheese to cool before snacking on them.

Smoke Time: 30 Mins

Smoke Temp: 350°

Smoked Brie with Roasted Peppers & Garlic

Craving a cheese with a bit of extra spice to it? While it won't set your mouth on fire, it will certainly make your taste buds warm. The garlic and smoke enhances the flavor too. Once done it's firm and creamy.

Ingredients:

1 (15 ounce) wheel double creme brie cheese

3 tsp. garlic, minced

3/4 cup extra virgin olive oil

2 green onions, white part only, finely chopped

1 (7 ounce) jar roasted red peppers, drained and diced

2 tsp. dried thyme or 2 tsp. fresh thyme

2 tsp. balsamic vinegar, well-aged

1 tbsp. cracked black pepper

1/2 tbsp. coarse kosher salt

Serves: 6
Preparation Time: 15 minutes

Directions:

1. Take the rind off of the wheel of brie. Set it aside.
2. In a saucepan, heat up the olive oil over a medium high heat. Add in the garlic.
3. Turn the heat down to medium low, and simmer for 15 minutes.
4. Take the saucepan from heat, and transfer the garlic oil to a small bowl to cool down.
5. Add in two tbsp. in another bowl. Add roasted pepper, black pepper, green onions, roasted red pepper, thyme, vinegar, and balsamic.
6. Season it with salt. Be sure to mix it up.
7. Spread the mixture on the top of the brie.
8. Place the cheese in the smoker.
9. Remove and serve with some bread.

Smoke Time: 12 Mins

Smoke Temp: 90°

Hot Smoked Brie with Roasted Grapes

Brie and roasted grapes combine to bring you a tasty snack. The creamy cheese mixed in with the warm, juicy grapes is a flavor combination you have to try. Get some crackers to place them on and you have a quick snack to enjoy.

Serves: 6
Preparation Time: 15 minutes

Directions:

1. Place cheese in the smoker.
2. Turn the oven on to 400 degrees. Bake the grapes for 20 minutes.
3. Serve with crackers or crusty bread.

Smoke Time: 40 Mins

Smoke Temp: 120°

Ingredients:

4 brie cheeses

500g red seedless grapes

Smoked Salmon Cream Cheese Ball

Ingredients:

4 to 6 oz. smoked salmon, cut
    into small pieces

16 oz. cream cheese, softened

1 cup shredded cheddar cheese

2 green onions, finely chopped

2 tbsp lemon juice

1 tbsp minced fresh dill

1 tsp garlic powder

1 tsp Old Bay Seasoning

salt and pepper to taste

1 cup finely chopped walnuts

A cheese ball is excellent for those times you want to have something to snack on. It's small, convenient, and best of all has salmon in it. So you know you're getting those extra nutrients your body needs while enjoying a creamy, crunchy snack.

Serves: 10

Preparation Time: 15 minutes

Directions:

1. Spread a large piece of plastic wrap on the counter.
2. In a large bowl, mix together all the ingredients. Roll it into a large ball.
3. Store it in the fridge for half an hour.
4. Place the cheese in the smoker. Afterwards, roll the cheese ball in a couple of walnuts. Enjoy with some crackers.

Smoke Time: 2 Hours

Smoke Temp: 90°

Smoked Salmon Frittata

Salmon is a classic favorite in the world of fish cuisine. Better yet, you can have this for dinner or lunch. The frittata gives the salmon a hint of creaminess while still allowing for you to enjoy the tender meat of the fish.

Serves: 8
Preparation Time: 10 minutes

Directions:

1. In a pan sauté the butter and onions. Do this for five minutes.

2. Get a large bowl, and beat the eggs. Add in pepper, heavy cream, salt, goat cheese, dill, smoked salmon, and scallions. Transfer to an aluminum pan. Pour the mixture of over the butter and onion mixture.

3. Place the pan in the smoker.

4. Once done serve the salmon frittata while it's still hot.

Smoke Time: 50 Mins

Smoke Temp: 350°

Ingredients:

1 medium onion, diced

1 tbsp. unsalted butter

12 extra-large eggs

1 cup heavy cream

4 ounces fresh goat cheese, such as Montrachet, crumbled

1/2 lb. smoked salmon, chopped

3 scallions, chopped, white and light green parts

3 tsp. chopped fresh dill

1 tbsp. kosher salt

1/2 tbsp. freshly ground black pepper

WANT TO KNOW HOW TO COOK THE WORLD'S MOST FLAVORFUL AND TENDER MEAT?

GET THE QUICKSTART GUIDE FREE!

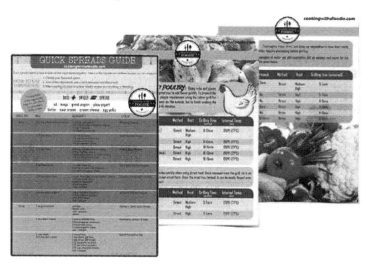

This book comes with a barbecue grilling quickstart guide which includes:

- Recipes for finger lickin' good sauces and rubs
- Time and temperature guide to cooking any type of meat
- More secrets and techniques straight from the pros
- All new upcoming high-quality guides

**GRAB YOUR FREEBIES NOW AT
SMOKEANDGRILLMEAT.COM**

Made in the USA
San Bernardino, CA
08 June 2016